PRAISE FOR *B2B MA… STRATEGY*

'Give a copy of this book to every B2B marketer you know. *B2B Marketing Strategy* is a siren call for marketers to stop behaving like tacticians, and to start leading marketing within their organizations. In this book, Heidi Taylor shows us how, adapting familiar models for today's B2B and illustrating the relevance of a solid foundation in the marketing fundamentals. She knows what she's talking about. Taylor is an award-winning B2B marketer and is a mentor to the next generation of marketing professionals. When she has something to say, we listen.'
Katryna Turner, Board Member, Business Marketing Club

'I've known Heidi Taylor for a number of years now, and she has proven herself to be a passionate exponent and enthusiast for excellence in B2B marketing. These attributes come across clearly in her book, where she bravely disassembles some key myths and fallacies that too often dominate thinking today, reasserts why many marketing challenges are perennials, and explains why we need to get back to the fundamentals of our profession. If you're a committed B2B marketer, this book is certain to challenge, inform and ultimately reinvigorate your approach – it's a thoroughly worthwhile investment in your career.'
Joel Harrison, Editor-in-Chief, *B2B Marketing*

'Heidi Taylor has written a book which should be mandatory reading for every B2B marketer looking to progress their career. Challenging yourself to think different, do different and be different can be very difficult but it's an important step in your career path if you want to successfully surf the B2B marketing tsunami of transformation that's been happening over the past few years. No doubt, this book will change your B2B marketing life (as it has already changed mine) and prepare you to become a greater B2B marketer.'
Stephane Antona, VP Marketing EMEA, Appian

'Packed full of insightful, thought-provoking ideas about contemporary B2B marketing practice and the need to stay focused on business outcomes rather than the latest management fads. This highly readable book provides a timely challenge to many of the taken-for-granted assumptions about how B2B marketing works

and what matters in the creation of customer and business value. The message is clear – only by changing how we think about B2B marketing can we change how we do B2B marketing. A definite recommendation for marketing students and sales and marketing professionals who want to make a real difference.'
Dr Paul R Johnston, Marketing Subject Group Leader, Sheffield Business School, Sheffield Hallam University

'Written by someone who has worked for over two decades across the B2B marketing landscape, this is an essential read for marketers of all levels. No hype, no fads; just straight talk, solid advice and practical examples of where and how B2B marketers need to apply their focus, energy and resources.'
Roberta de Lima, Head of UK Marketing, BAI Communications

'A call to arms for B2B marketers everywhere, this book is a vital read for any practitioner keen to prove the value that marketing provides to their business. Heidi Taylor has tackled a long-overdue issue in B2B marketing head on, highlighting exactly why strategy and purpose should always drive tactical marketing activities.'
Danny Jack, Head of Marketing and Corporate Communications, TradeRiver

'Heidi is the best marketer I've ever come across; she excels because of her innate understanding of what drives and grows a business, and makes that her starting point, only then creating the marketing strategy and plans that will deliver on that organization's objectives. This book reflects her insight and experience, and it will be as useful to the public and charity sectors as it is to business. It helps us think about how we need to influence and engage other organizations in order to achieve our objectives.'
Dame Julie Mellor, Chair, The Young Foundation, and former Partner at PwC

'Heidi Taylor has produced an essential must-read modern handbook for today's B2B marketers. The book is admirably accessible, while at the same time being in depth and analytical. In it Taylor provides an inspiring set of tools, examples and methodologies to suit the breadth of marketing challenges faced by practitioners. Perhaps most importantly, Taylor reminds us throughout the vastly informative chapters of the essential plumb line of customer focus that must be at the heart of every marketing strategy. This book provides a necessary and timely reminder for all marketers, in a world obsessed with broadcasting in all its forms, of their responsibility, and the universal human need not only to be heard, but listened to.'
Lisa Lavia, Managing Director, Noise Abatement Society

'Heidi Taylor is a true B2B marketing professional with a strong understanding of the principles of B2B marketing and what is required to ensure brands thrive. She delivers sound reasoning on how marketing can deliver real value to the business. More than ever before in the B2B environment, the marketing department must take centre stage and be pulled from the back room to the boardroom. This is a must-read for any B2B marketer or organization.'
Jay Neale, Managing Director, The Agency Works

'This book is a great read. Heidi Taylor's back-to-basics approach is timely given the constant flow of shiny new tools that threaten to distract B2B marketers. *B2B Marketing Strategy* is strategic and thought-provoking yet gives practical advice that can be acted on straight away.'
Polly Barton, Head of Global Business Development, Bovill

'As a business owner and recruiter within the marketing arena, I have read a number of books on B2B marketing and am usually left feeling overwhelmed by jargon or underwhelmed by lack of meaningful content. Heidi Taylor's book is different, and offers valuable insights for any level of marketer. Heidi cuts to the chase and gets to the heart of the matter eloquently and succinctly. This book clearly spells out the principles, challenges and future of B2B marketing in an ever-changing landscape, and is a highly recommended read for anyone serious about ensuring their marketing delivers results in the 21st century.'
Simone Timcke, Director, Anthem Consulting, B2B Marketing Recruitment

'Heidi Taylor has expertly distilled all her years of B2B marketing experience and knowledge in a book that accurately reflects the issues and opportunities that affect modern marketing professionals. Her 3D Marketing System should become the adopted method for B2B marketing.'
Terry Hewett, Chairman, Zest

'A vital book for today's B2B marketers who want to stand out from the competition and become leaders in their organizations by thinking, doing and being *different*! The need to return to marketing fundamentals as the enabling foundation is extremely well articulated and is applicable to all B2B professionals.'
Sylvie Jolly, Founder and Director, Oceane Communication

'A refreshingly thought-provoking and insightful read that will have you thinking different about current thinking!'
Yetunde Hofmann, Leadership and Change expert, and Visiting Fellow at The University of Reading, Henley Business School

B2B Marketing Strategy

Differentiate, develop and deliver lasting customer engagement

Heidi Taylor

First published in Great Britain and the United States in 2018 by Kogan Page Limited

2nd Floor, 45 Gee Street
London
EC1V3RS
United Kingdom

c/o Martin P Hill Consulting
122 W 27th St, 10th Floor
New York, NY 10001
USA

4737/23 Ansari Road
Daryaganj
New Delhi 110002
India

www.koganpage.com

ISBN 978 0 7494 8106 3
E-ISBN 978 0 7494 8107 0

British Library Cataloguing-in-Publication Data

A CIP record for this book is available from the British Library.

Library of Congress Cataloging-in-Publication Data

Names: Taylor, Heidi (Marketing consultant), author.
Title: B2B marketing strategy : differentiate, develop and deliver lasting customer engagement / Heidi Taylor.
Description: London ; New York : Kogan Page, 2017. | Includes index.
Identifiers: LCCN 2017026095 (print) | LCCN 2017043331 (ebook) | ISBN 9780749481070 (ebook) | ISBN 9780749481063 (pbk.)
Subjects: LCSH: Industrial marketing.
Classification: LCC HF5415.1263 (ebook) | LCC HF5415.1263 .T39 2017 (print) | DDC 658.8/04–dc23
LC record available at https://lccn.loc.gov/2017026095

Typeset by Integra Software Services, Pondicherry
Print production managed by Jellyfish
Printed and bound by Ashford Colour Press Ltd, Gosport, Hampshire

This book is dedicated to all
B2B marketers who strive to think,
do and be different in their lives as well as their work.

CONTENTS

List of figures and tables xii
About the author xiii
Acknowledgements xiv

Introduction 1

PART ONE Think different 7

01 Change happens: the seismic shift in our B2B marketing environment 9

Seismic shift 9
The engagement continuum 12
Words influence perception: client versus customer in B2B marketing 14
Emotions in B2B marketing 16
The rise of social media 19
Who moved my cheese? 20
How are B2B marketers responding to change? 21

02 All that glitters: B2B marketing's obsession with the latest tools and tactics 23

'Marketing myopia' 24
Traditional versus new (digital) marketing 27
Magpie mania: where should we focus our marketing? 33

03 Thinking different about B2B marketing 43

Essential steps to *think different* 47

PART TWO Do different 49

04 Getting back to B2B marketing basics 51

The four fundamentals for B2B marketing success 51
Who am I? The brand conundrum in B2B 53
The strategy imperative 59
Customer engagement: winning hearts and minds 65
The end of ROI as we know it? 68

05 An introduction to 3D marketing 73

A 3D Marketing System for Strategy and Planning 73
Applying 3D marketing to business strategy 88

06 Doing different for B2B marketing 91

A return to marketing 93
Essential steps to *do different* 94

PART THREE Be different 99

07 What is the purpose of marketing? 101

Let's talk about lead generation 102
The three stonecutters revisited 103
A threefold purpose for marketing 105
Revisiting the marketing mix 106
Not enough C-words: the dearth of creativity in B2B 117
Not 'boring' B2B: three inspiring B2B case studies 118

08 What makes a great B2B marketer? 123

Four essential qualities of great marketers 123
The seven behaviours of the most successful marketers 125
The qualifications debate 129
A career in marketing? Advice to my younger self 139

09 The leadership dilemma in B2B marketing 141

Should marketing have a seat on the board in B2B? 141
Why should anyone be led by you? 142
What do our CEOs want from marketing? 147
What makes a B2B marketing leader? 148
Becoming B2B marketing leaders 149

10 Customer engagement for the social era 157

Six rules for social engagement 158
Taking a big idea to market 165
Five top tips for developing a big idea 167

11 Being different in B2B marketing 175

Being B2B marketers 177
Essential steps to *be different* 179

Conclusion: being better B2B marketers 183

References and further reading 187
Index 195

LIST OF FIGURES AND TABLES

Figures

FIGURE 1.1 The sales funnel yesterday and today 12
FIGURE 1.2 The engagement continuum 13
FIGURE 1.3 Wheel of emotion 18
FIGURE 1.4 The handwriting on the wall 20
FIGURE 4.1 The Golden Circle 54
FIGURE 4.2 Marketing process, inside-out 55
FIGURE 4.3 Marketing process, outside-in 56
FIGURE 4.4 Purpose, mission, vision and goal 57
FIGURE 5.1 3D Marketing System for B2B Strategy and Planning 74
FIGURE 5.2 3D marketing strategy 75
FIGURE 5.3 3D go-to-market ecosystem 83
FIGURE 5.4 3D marketing planning framework 84
FIGURE 7.1 The 4Ps of the marketing mix 107
FIGURE 7.2 The 7Ps of the services marketing mix and the 4Cs of the customer-focused marketing mix 108
FIGURE 7.3 The 4Ps for B2B marketing 112
FIGURE 8.1 Time management for B2B marketers 128
FIGURE 9.1 SMART objectives 155

Tables

TABLE 3.1 Think different Q&A 48
TABLE 5.1 The strategic narrative 80
TABLE 5.2 Example of the strategic narrative 81
TABLE 6.1 Do different Q&A 96
TABLE 11.1 Be different Q&A 180

ABOUT THE AUTHOR

Heidi Taylor has been a B2B marketer her entire career, spanning 25 years and multiple industries, from IT hardware and software, to telecommunications and professional services. She is a consultant, speaker and prolific blogger with a passion for working with the next generation of marketers to ensure they have the perspective and tools to achieve their goals and maximize their abilities in a continually changing business landscape. Her expertise is in strategy and planning, and in creating powerful integrated marketing programmes and campaigns that help organizations engage meaningfully with their customers.

She is a sought-after speaker at marketing conferences in the UK and internationally, and regularly contributes to industry journals in print and online. She also comments on B2B marketing-related topics in her blog at www.heidi-taylor.com/blog, on LinkedIn at www.uk.linkedin.com/in/heiditaylor1 and on Twitter @TaylorMadeInKew.

Heidi was named by *B2B Marketing*'s editor-in-chief as a top 10 B2B marketer to follow on Twitter and as a top 25 UK B2B Marketing Influencer by Onalytica. She is a former Chartered Institute of Marketing's Marketer of the Year and a Professional Services Marketing category winner in their Marketing Excellence Awards.

She holds a BA in Fine Arts and an MBA in International Marketing. She lives in London, England, and consults widely with professional services and other B2B organizations to develop marketing strategy and integrated marketing programmes that engage customers in new ways. www.heidi-taylor.com.

ACKNOWLEDGEMENTS

I had been blogging about B2B marketing for a number of years when I started to think about writing a book. Blogging was my way of thinking about and working through the marketing challenges I was facing in my working life and I was astounded at the response I received from my blogs.

But writing a book is very different from writing a blog, and I just couldn't seem to begin. My utmost thanks goes to Tim Hughes, author of *Social Selling*, whom I met at a B2B marketing networking event. Tim not only encouraged me to write a book, he introduced me to his publisher who has become my publisher. My special thanks go to Kogan Page commissioning editor, Jenny Volich, who believed in the themes I wanted to address and helped me through the book proposal process. Thanks also to my development editor, Charlotte Owen, whose guidance and encouragement kept me going through the dark days of winter.

My community and network of B2B marketers – both online and offline – helped me to further explore and refine the themes in this book through continuing discussion and debate (and often raucous laughter) in regular forums like the BMC. It is their everyday experiences of marketing in B2B that have helped to inform my thinking and added depth to my own experience of working in and with such organizations.

I'd particularly like to thank some very special people. Dave Stevens of www.davestevensnow.com and Brian Macreadie and Ash Coleman-Smith of Berwin Leighton Paisner shared their stories with me and allowed me to publicly share those stories here. Yetunde Hofmann – leadership and change expert, and visiting fellow at the University of Reading Henley Business School – sparked my thinking about B2B marketing leadership and how we deal with change. I'm especially grateful to Dame Julie Mellor, who relentlessly pushed me outside of my comfort zone all those years ago, and is a continuing source of friendship and inspiration.

Lastly, but never last in my heart, I'd like to thank the friends and family who supported and encouraged me on this incredible journey.

Introduction

It's the middle of the 21st century, digital is pervasive, content is everywhere and business-to-business (B2B) marketing has come a long way.

Or has it?

We've adopted new tools and technologies, come to grips with new channels and done a lot of work creating more and more content for our customers to consume. But are we really thinking and doing much different from what we've always thought and done in B2B marketing? And are we really any different from our competitors?

The commercial landscape has suddenly shifted right under our feet. We've hardly been aware of it, but our business customers have brought their consumer buying behaviours into the B2B world. We are living, working and doing business in an increasingly commoditized world where there is very little differentiation between our products and services, the organizations we work for or our competitors. Bigger, better, faster, cheaper is no longer a compelling enough reason for our customers to buy from us.

Yet the bulk of our B2B marketing effort continues to be based on features, benefits and price, pushing out our messages and our content in mostly the same ways, albeit through new (digital) channels.

A lot of marketers tell me that what they do has changed so much over the past few years that they are really worried about keeping up, and that, in particular, they feel so besieged by all the new technology that they don't know what to focus on or where to begin. And this is where B2B marketing is breaking down. What we do as marketers – the actual outputs – may change with the times and technology, but how we do it does not. And the only way to keep on top of an ever-changing and increasingly fast-paced world is to continually go back to the marketing basics.

Understanding what drives and grows a business, a relentless focus on the customer, delivering what the customer finds of value and finding relevant customer insight based on the available data, as well as creative ideas and design, are what great marketers have relied on for decades. What's new is the technology that has enabled our customers to take control of the buying process and the number of new channels and tactics that marketers need to master in order to be where our customers are. And marketers are overwhelmed by what appears to be an insurmountable task – changing the way they 'do marketing'.

But technology is not the challenge; there will *always* be new technology – think about the transition from word-of-mouth marketing to newsprint, radio, telephone, television and the internet. Each of these channels enabled customers to access and consume information in new ways, which in turn gave marketers new opportunities to communicate and engage with their customers. Today is essentially no different; the real challenge for B2B marketers isn't in the addition of new tactics and channels to the marketing toolkit, nor is it in the execution. Because while a lot has changed, the fundamentals of marketing remain the same.

The real challenge is that in our headlong frenzy to become 'digital' we have become too focused on the wrong things. Like our businesses, we are too caught up in what we do – the tactics – instead of the outcomes we want and need to achieve with our customers.

Marketing at the core

The best organizations are driven by marketing, not sales. I'm not trivializing sales – indeed, without the revenue brought in by the sales teams and the profits that result, any business will fail. But the most successful companies are successful because they function with marketing at their core. They understand that brand equity matters, that marketing builds both company and customer value, for the short and long term, and is uniquely placed to be the voice of the customer throughout the organization.

But in B2B, marketing continues to have limited business impact. In particular, sales and marketing have traditionally been separate and siloed functions, with marketing being an activity that is done *to* the business instead of *with* the business. The CMO Council found that as much as 40 per cent of salespeople's time is spent creating their own messaging and materials to use with their customers (Davies, 2015a). Furthermore, according to an Econsultancy blog post (Davies, 2015b), a shocking 70–90 per cent of marketing content produced by B2B companies is not used by the sales teams or anyone else in their organizations.

This will sound very familiar to many B2B marketers. However, even though throughout this book I discuss marketing in the context of B2B, in reality, many of the principles are relevant for marketers in all organizations, whether they be consumer, business or non-profit, small, medium or large. Because without marketing at the core, it is becoming increasingly difficult to compete in today's social era.

Think different, do different, be different

The overall purpose of this book is to challenge and inspire B2B marketers and their organizations to *think different*, *do different* and *be different* in what I have just called the 'social era'. But I'm not just referring to social media; I'm describing the world in which we live and do business as a fundamentally social place. Because ever since we lived in caves, we've come together in social groups to live our lives, to collaborate, to work and to share. As humans, we *are* social beings. And this is the context that we must incorporate into our marketing.

Jonathan MacDonald, speaker and founder of the Thought Expansion Network, said 'this very moment is the slowest pace of change we will ever experience' (MacDonald, 2014). For this very reason, in this increasingly fast-paced business environment, it is more important than ever to revisit our marketing roots, learn and relearn the fundamentals of our profession, and start to *think different* about what we do and how we do it.

In addition, every day I hear from marketers who tell me how busy they are, how they are constantly pressured to do more and more, with steadily decreasing resources. Yet they also continue to tell me that their businesses don't really value what they do. My response is: if your business does not value what you do, then *do* (something) *different*, something they *will* value!

And finally, we must stop doing what we've always done, just because it's always worked out all right for us. We must stop doing more and more of the same old 'stuff' without really understanding what we are trying to achieve. We must stop focusing on our organizations and what we sell, and focus instead on our customers and what they want and need from us.

We must *be different* from what we've ever been, because we are doing business in a world that is unlike any that has come before. This is the joy and the challenge of marketing. But in our tumultuous rush to 'become digital' we have drifted further and further away from our roots as marketers. While the world in which we do business may have fundamentally changed, the core principles of marketing have not.

Getting back to basics: the marketing fundamentals

It all starts with Strategy. *Strategy is the foundation for everything*. It articulates the approach we take towards our markets and provides both clarity and purpose around what we do – and more importantly, what we don't do. A marketing strategy organizes our thinking and thus our actions around what is most important for our business, enabling us to develop and execute marketing plans that differentiate us from our competitors.

But strategy is hard; and it takes more than tactical marketing expertise – it takes a deep understanding of our customers and our business.

In this book I introduce my 3D Marketing System, which provides a framework and process for marketing strategy and planning. It's simple, but not easy! It's a tool to guide B2B marketers on their journey towards becoming truly memorable in the hearts and minds of their customers, creating lasting engagement, long after any marketing campaign is over.

Because strategy isn't just words on a page; strategy is the touchstone that every marketer throughout our organizations needs to understand, and against which every single marketing activity must be aligned and measured.

Changing our perspective – the three fallacies of B2B marketing

1. Digital has forever and fundamentally changed marketing's very foundations, so that its function and purpose are nothing like what has come before.
2. The marketing plan *is* the marketing strategy.
3. The purpose of marketing is lead generation.

These are the three fallacies that are continuing to dominate B2B marketing thinking and they are damaging us as a profession. In this book I confront, explore and irrevocably refute them, providing practical advice and best-practice case study examples to help us change our marketing perspective.

I continue to be concerned about the direction that B2B marketing is taking and what we are neglecting to teach our young marketers. I attend conferences, roundtables and other events where the conversation has not fundamentally changed over the past three years or more. I hear the same frustrations and the same excuses – we don't have the right people or the right tools, we don't have a big enough budget, the data isn't telling us what the business wants or needs to know about the impact marketing is having, our legacy systems won't integrate with the technology, there's so much noise out in the market I'm not reaching our customers, we're so busy all the time... I could go on and on.

But marketers have always faced these challenges in B2B. And we have to stop making excuses for what we can't do and start to focus on becoming better marketers.

Differentiate, develop and deliver for lasting customer engagement

What is the role and purpose of B2B marketing? Why do we do what we do and how do we do it? These questions lie at the heart of marketing thinking. Our job is fundamentally about engaging our customers in meaningful ways that ultimately differentiate our organizations, our people, and our products and services from our competitors. We do this by developing marketing campaigns and programmes that deliver value for our customers and an outcome for our organizations.

This is a major shift in marketing thinking for B2B – from a focus on what we sell (inside-out) to a relentless customer perspective (outside-in). To facilitate this shift, I've structured this book into three sections:

- *Think different* is the heart of Part One and explores the first of my three fallacies. This section concentrates on the shift that has taken place in our marketing environment and where we need to place our attention in order to *differentiate* ourselves in an increasingly undifferentiated world.
- *Do different* is the focus for Part Two. This section takes a look at the fundamentals of marketing, which have not changed, but to which we must bring new perspectives. It also introduces my 3D Marketing System, which takes the reader through a six-step process to *develop* marketing strategy and the plans that support that strategy.
- *Be different* is the soul of Part Three. This final section explores many of the misconceptions that continue to plague B2B marketing and provides an action plan so that we can *deliver* lasting customer engagement in this social era of marketing.

Because, ultimately, our role as B2B marketers – if we do our jobs well – is to make our brands and our people memorable in the hearts and minds of our customers long after any marketing campaign or sales promotion is over.

PART ONE
Think different

FALLACY 1

Digital has forever and fundamentally changed marketing's very foundations, so that its function and purpose are nothing like what has come before.

---

76 per cent of people feel that marketing has changed more in the past 2 years than in the previous 50.
ADOBE, 2016

Change happens 01

The seismic shift in our B2B marketing environment

At the end of Chapter 3, I use Apple's iconic 'Think Different' campaign of 1997 as a case study for the three fundamentals of marketing: brand, strategy and customers. Whether you are a consumer or business marketer, the Apple story remains a compelling one, and serves as a potent reminder of what forms the core principles of the marketing profession.

But, wait a minute, it's been 20 years since that campaign and a lot has changed – or has it? We are operating in a commercial landscape that has shaken B2B marketing's foundations to its roots, but what exactly has changed? Is it marketing itself or merely the environment in which we do business?

Seismic shift

Let's put this into perspective.

Before the vast changes in technology that led to the ubiquity of 'digital', marketing was all about our organizations and what we sell, pushing out our messages to a largely passive audience through what were primarily broadcast and print channels. This built awareness of our brands – which were represented by a single corporate spokesperson who was the voice of that brand – and enabled our organizations to control both the medium and the message for our brands.

Today, it is our customers who are in control. The sheer amount of information that our customers are able to access across such a wide variety of channels, combined with the rise of social media within B2B, means that our customers are not passive receivers of our messages any more, and they are certainly no longer silent.

This requires us to move away from one-way broadcast channels (and it doesn't matter whether they are 'digital' or 'traditional') to multi-way, dynamic *engagement* channels in order to create impact and differentiation in the hearts and minds of our customers. And we simply can't do this through a single 'brand voice' any more but need to involve the multiplicity of voices that are our entire organizations.

We know all this. But have we really embraced it? Are we thinking and doing much different from what we've always thought and done in B2B marketing?

Digital is now a pervasive part of our lives and we've got to stop worrying about where digital ends and so-called 'traditional' marketing begins. Digital has, in effect, become invisible, like electricity, powering our world, taken for granted.

Sure, we have a lot of new channels, and a whole host of new tools, all of which makes marketing a lot more complicated and interesting. But we're concentrating on the wrong things. We're concentrating on the tasks and the technology in and of themselves, instead of their relevance to marketing; in other words, how these new tools enable us to better communicate with and engage our customers.

And this is the real shift that we need to make in B2B marketing: to 'Think Different', bigger, more holistically, and from a true customer perspective.

The customer journey has forever and fundamentally changed

It won't come as a surprise to anyone that there has been a fundamental change in the customer buying journey. We are living in an increasingly complex multi-channel world where B2B buying decisions are now being influenced and made long before a salesperson even makes contact.

In fact, our B2B customers tell us they don't want to be 'sold to' any more. I've sat in customer meetings with my salespeople and been bluntly told that they're happy to meet with us, but please, don't try to sell anything. So, what do we have to talk to our customers about if we can't talk about what we sell?

There are a lot of statistics that have been bandied about over the past few years, but most B2B marketers are broadly in agreement:

- nine out of ten of our customers say they will find us when they're ready;
- up to 80 per cent are starting their buying journey with a web search;
- and more than half are already two-thirds through their decision-making process before they even talk to a salesperson.

And, in most of our B2B sectors, our customers are predominantly invisible to us until they're ready to make a purchase.

Today's technology is enabling our customers to access huge amounts of information in so many diverse ways, and as a result they want to engage with us and our organizations in fundamentally different ways. They're bringing their buying behaviours from the consumer world into the business world and are now being influenced in their buying decisions through the information they find online, often engaging directly with others in the marketplace. This is giving our customers unprecedented control of the conversations we might want to have with them and is profoundly changing what we do as marketers.

Beyond the sales funnel – marketing's role just got a whole lot more complicated

Once upon a time – a mere decade ago – the buyer journey in B2B was relatively straightforward and linear, and marketing's job was to fill the top of the sales funnel by creating awareness of our brands and driving interest for our products and services. To do this, a B2B marketer's toolkit consisted almost solely of PR activity, trade shows and events, and product or service collateral, with perhaps some product and industry-specific advertising added to the mix.

The traditional sales and marketing approach pushed these products or services to customers along this linear funnel and focused on lead generation and qualification, the bid or proposal, negotiation of terms and closing of the sale. Funnel metrics kept track of from where a sale would most likely come and when, enabling sales to remain on track for achieving or exceeding their targets within the specified timeframe set by the business (Figure 1.1).

The problem is that today's B2B customers no longer buy this way. Our customers are increasingly bringing their consumer buying behaviours into the B2B world. And sales tracking alone does not provide the business with any insight into what is driving these buying behaviours.

This dramatic shift in the buyer journey means that marketing now 'owns' more of the sales funnel than ever before, with sales focused on, well, closing the sale, a shift that many in our B2B organizations have not quite got to grips with. Yet, we still tend to think of the B2B customer journey in terms of this funnel. We depend upon marketing to have done their 'brand awareness' job so that when our salespeople come calling our customers will be interested in hearing about what we have to sell.

Figure 1.1 The sales funnel yesterday and today

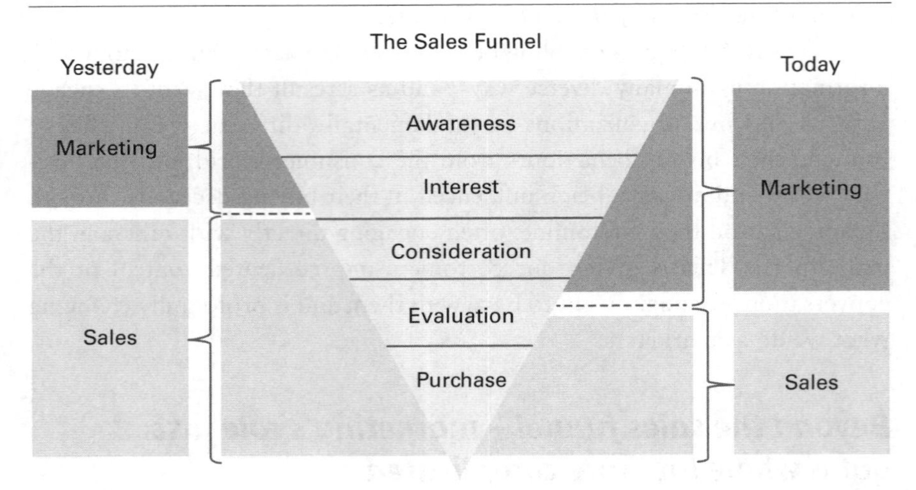

In many ways, the funnel is still a useful model and it remains an important tool for both sales and marketing. The funnel is the foundation for a business to understand its sales pipeline as well as for developing and delivering its marketing strategy. It creates the roadmap for the buying journey so that we as marketers can decide what outcomes we want to achieve at each stage in the journey, where to focus our marketing efforts, what tactics to use and what marketing success looks like.

Yet it's an outdated model for looking at the customer buying cycle. First, the customer buying journey is no longer this simple or linear. But most importantly, the funnel model is overly concerned with 'what we sell' instead of what the customer actually wants and needs.

The engagement continuum

I now look at the customer buying journey in B2B as an engagement continuum, where there are multiple potential touchpoints for both traditional and new marketing activity. Because if our customers no longer want to be sold to, we have to completely change our perspective and think not only about where along the buying journey we need to have a presence, but how we can engage with our customers *before* their buying journey even begins (Figure 1.2). (I will explore this concept of engagement before customers may even be thinking about a purchase further in Part Three.)

Figure 1.2 The engagement continuum

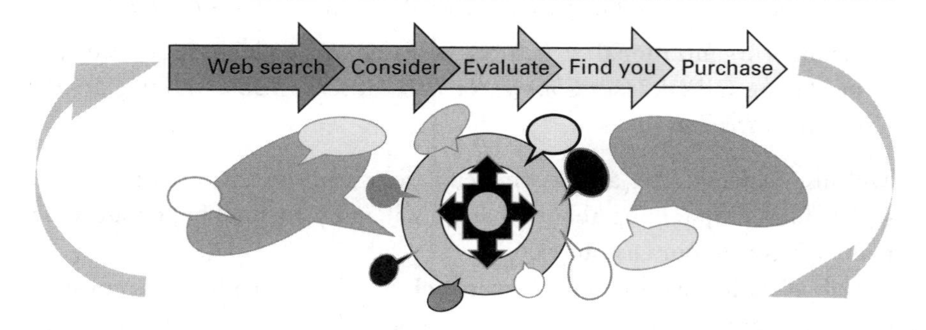

But even this doesn't adequately explain the buying journey. Because in reality, this journey is rarely linear any more and increasingly involves more than a single decision-making authority. This is challenging for B2B sales teams, who often have long-standing relationships with those individual decision-makers. And the more complex, costly or risky a purchase, the more people will be involved in the decision-making process. Furthermore, our B2B buyers have their own influencers across their organizations – as well as influencers outside of it – who may well be drawn in to the buying journey. They continually veer off the continuum, connect with their social networks, revise their needs and perceptions, go back online, source specific information, opinions and advice, go back and discuss with their internal stakeholders – both those who will have a say in the final purchase and those who will use the product or service – *at any point during the journey* and long before they ever make contact with a salesperson.

In the February 2015 issue of the *McKinsey Quarterly*, Oskar Lingqvist, Candace Lun Plotkin and Jennifer Stanley spoke about how B2B companies across industries as diverse as industrial-equipment manufacturers, software firms, professional services firms, telecom providers and basic materials companies were already moving towards a 'journey-based sales strategy'. This approach for B2B sales makes a lot of sense for B2B marketing as well, including the three recommendations that McKinsey makes for enabling this move (see my thoughts in italics):

- Chart decision journeys by customer segment and drill down on customer expectations and needs at each stage of the journey (*engage your customer at multiple touchpoints along their journey and integrate into a single customer experience*).

- Tackle the difficult process of reallocating sales and marketing resources to the activities most likely to influence decisions (*do less but do it better*).
- Change organizational structures to ramp up collaboration between marketing and sales (*see Chapter 9 where I discuss B2B marketing organizational structure*).

McKinsey's perspective and recommendations reinforce the notion that we simply must stop talking about what we sell and start thinking about what really matters to our customers.

I often tell a story about a salesperson I once knew in a business consulting organization. They had previously done well-received work for a very large client and were invited in to pitch for a new piece of large, long-term consulting work. They went in and did the pitch, which they thought went really well because they thought they'd come up with a unique and powerful solution to the customer business need, only to be told that they'd come second and lost the work. When they asked the prospective customer the reason why, the customer told them that while their proposal was extremely interesting, it wasn't what they had asked for. The salesperson told me that they couldn't understand it, that the customer didn't really know what would solve their problem, that what they had asked for wasn't going to solve their problem, and their solution was the one the customer really needed.

The point of this story is that it didn't matter whether this consultant really had the better solution or not, they approached the pitch so fired up with this great idea they had for transforming the customer's business – what they were selling – that they hadn't taken into account what this would look like from the customer's perspective. They had also neglected to engage with the customer since the last piece of work they had done for them. So, while the consultant's own thinking about the challenges the customer was facing had been moving in a particular direction, that thinking was not aligned to the customer's perceptions of that challenge.

Words influence perception: client versus customer in B2B marketing

This story also illustrates that despite all the talk about customer focus, customer centricity, customer engagement and customer experience these days, many of us – and not just in marketing – don't understand what this truly means. We are still too focused on what we do – our products and services, our tasks and our outputs – instead of continually asking ourselves a critical question: 'Does this matter to our customers?'

Knowing our customers has never been more important. As marketers, we know this, it's a given, because B2B is so heavily relationship driven. And yet, most of us in B2B marketing typically think of our customers as organizations and job titles.

Invariably, when I'm reviewing B2B marketing plans, the customer being targeted is someone in the C-suite – traditionally, the chief executive officer (CEO), the chief financial officer (CFO) and the chief operations officer (COO), but may also include the chief technology officer (CTO), the chief information officer (CIO) and even the chief marketing officer (CMO) – the group of senior executives who are the decision-making leadership team for a company. Yet, as we've just explored, there are many more individuals at all levels throughout an organization who are involved in the decision-making process.

How well do we in B2B marketing know our customers? Do we know who they are and do we actually think from their perspective?

You may have noticed that I've been using the word 'customer' when talking about the people we do business with in B2B. It varies depending upon which industry we're in, and whether we market and sell tangible products or more intangible services, but – particularly in professional services – we tend to call the people we do business with our 'clients'. Have we ever given much thought to why this is and what it might mean?

I ask because I'm continually fascinated by the ways in which the language we use, the words we speak, impact how we think and behave. A lot of the language we use is idiosyncratic to our B2B markets, and this language is a major influence on our perceptions and perspectives.

The dictionary defines client and customer as follows:

- A **client** is 'a person or organization using the services of a lawyer or other professional person or company'.
- While a **customer** is 'a person who buys goods or services from a shop or business'.

A client *uses*. A customer *buys*. It's a subtle but important distinction in how we think about and engage with the people we do business with in B2B.

Especially within the professional services environment – where we speak solely about 'clients' – we have somehow completely got away from the concepts of buying and selling, as if those activities are vulgar or beneath us, as if money never changes hands and we magically win work. We talk about 'decision-makers' instead of 'buyers', we speak of 'relationships' instead of 'sales'. We focus on bids and pitches, our expertise and experience, and make very specific assumptions about what drives our customers when we think of them as 'clients'.

We may not be entirely aware of these assumptions, but they are insidious. Most commonly, when we think in terms of clients, we are making the (often unconscious) assumption that they have already bought our product or service, and thus the sales and marketing job is done, even if they are still a target. Furthermore, there may still be the implementation and service phases to deliver over time, but these clients are now 'using' our products or services. I've heard these same clients complain again and again that too often, once they've chosen a supplier or awarded the work – in other words, purchased the product or service – they never again hear from the (often) very senior (sales)person who nurtured and sold to them in the first place. Their relationship with the supplier organization is then left to the delivery/implementation/service teams, who are mostly too junior to build and maintain the kinds of relationships these senior business people require. These relationships are just one part of the entire customer experience that will influence future buying behaviours.

We must realize that our 'clients' are customers who continue to 'buy' from us long after the sale has been made and the contract has been signed. And the drivers for those buying decisions are often not what we may think. Because buying decisions in B2B – and even in professional services – are fundamentally emotional decisions. These decisions may be justified and rationalized with facts and stats and data, but ultimately our customers don't just buy our products and services, they buy *us* and all that we represent to them on an emotional level. And by continuing to speak about our 'clients', the conversations we have and the stories we tell become conversations and stories about us and what we do, instead of about the issues and things that really matter to our 'customers'.

Emotions in B2B marketing

Historically, B2B organizations and their marketing functions have operated in the belief that their customers make purchasing decisions based solely on logic and reason, and are not influenced by emotion in the same way as B2C purchases. Yet over the past few years we've come to understand that emotion plays a bigger role in B2B behaviour than we imagined. The more complex, costly or risky a purchase, the more emotions come into play, because there is so much more at stake for the individual and organization making the purchase.

Yet in B2B, we get so caught up in what our organizations sell that we lose sight of what we're really trying to achieve through our marketing activity, which is ultimately about engaging with our customers in meaningful ways. *Emotions* provide the foundation for that meaning; so, we need to create content, tell stories and have conversations that are not about the products or services we sell, but about the big issues that are really important and personal to our customers. It's these issues that bring the human element to what we do, make conversations more meaningful and build relationships that last, enabling us to engage with our customers in ways that will linger in their hearts and minds long after any sales promotion or marketing campaign is over.

Robert Plutchik was a psychologist and professor emeritus at the Albert Einstein School of Medicine in New York City. His theory of emotion is considered one of the most influential classification approaches for general emotional responses, with eight primary emotions – anger, fear, sadness, disgust, surprise, anticipation, trust and joy. Each of these emotions has a polar opposite: fear and anger; joy and sadness; surprise and anticipation; and trust and disgust.

Plutchik created a colour wheel of emotion to illustrate the relationships among the emotions and their varying levels of intensity – for example, anger ranges from annoyance to rage. This breadth of emotion is illustrated in my adaptation of Plutchik's wheel (Figure 1.3) and it gives us some insight into the many and diverse emotions that consciously or subconsciously influence B2B buying decisions. But it also raises some fascinating questions: for example, interest is on the wheel, but not indifference; and there is no representation of greed, envy or pride.

Specifically for B2B, many of these emotions can be translated into drivers around:

- **progression** – the need to get ahead or gain an advantage over a competitor;
- **recognition** – advance a career or receive praise;
- **prevention** – remain secure in one's job or avoid threats and losses to the company.

Of course, there are others... such as stimulation, control and compliance. But my point is that we as marketers really need to get to grips with these drivers, and tap into them with our marketing activity.

Figure 1.3 Wheel of emotion

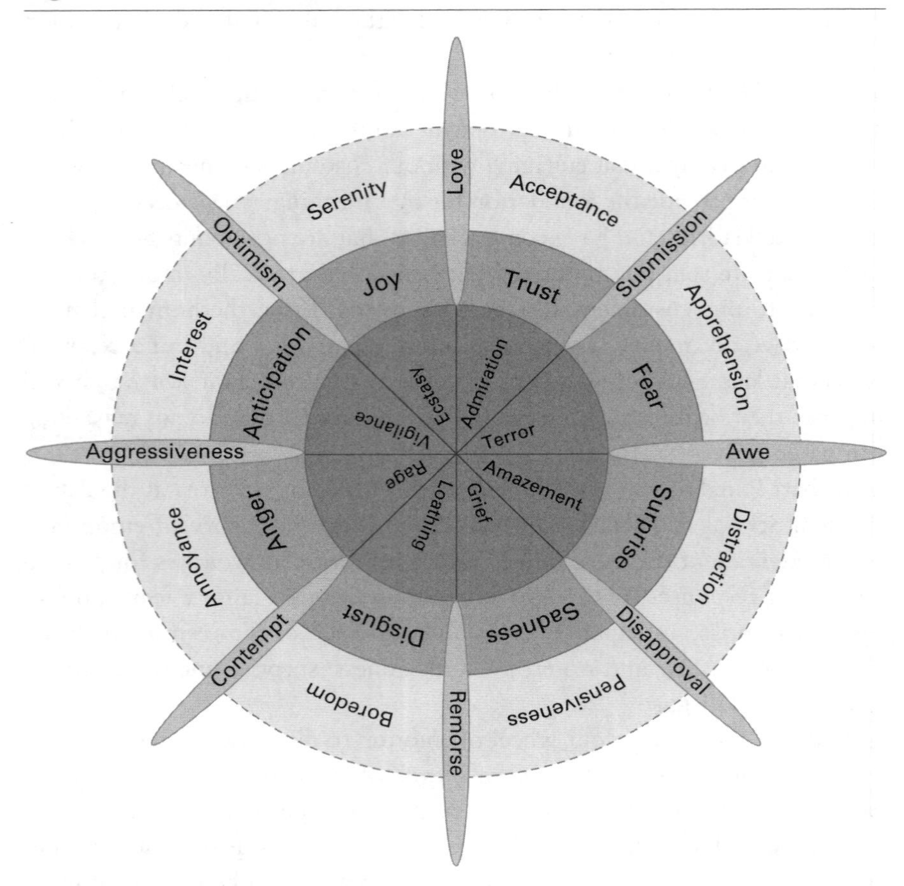

SOURCE Adapted from Plutchik (2001)

Because our customers don't just want to buy great products and services. They want to buy from people and organizations that they like to do business with, whose values align to their own, with whom they can build long-term lasting relationships and with whom they can really feel connected on an emotional level.

As the great poet Maya Angelou once said:

> People will forget what you said
>
> People will forget what you did
>
> But people will never forget how you made them feel.

To connect with our customers' hearts as well as their minds we need to engage with them not on our terms – from the perspective of what we sell, but on theirs – by understanding the issues that really matter to them. This is how we create differentiation in an undifferentiated world. And this is our real job as marketers, to find that emotional connection with our customers.

The rise of social media

Social media has become such a ubiquitous part of both our personal and professional lives that we forget how recent a phenomenon social media really is. Facebook, shortly followed by Twitter, may have launched more than a decade ago, but most sources I've seen tend to agree that it was only in 2010 that social media began to become mainstream, with broad business adoption coming even later.

There's no doubt that social media has fundamentally and forever changed how we connect with people. Yet many of us in B2B – and especially in professional services – have had a tough time getting to grips with social media in any meaningful way. Even today, the majority of us are still using social media as merely another channel through which to push out our sales and marketing messages.

Yet social media provides us with far more than another sales and marketing channel; it has given marketing the opportunity to think very differently about our customers and how we engage with them at a strategic level. While we can debate the returns of social media for achieving our wider organizational goals and objectives, as well as the merits and metrics for growing our brands and generating leads compared to other, more traditional channels, the single most important thing is that social media is compelling our organizations to change our perspective from 'inside-out' to 'outside-in'.

Most companies start with what they do – the product or service they are selling. They then go on to describe how great that product or service is, and spend a lot of sales and marketing time and budget on why their customers should buy it. This is what I mean by an 'inside-out' perspective.

But this social era calls for a different approach; our customers call for a different approach. Our customers now expect us to engage with them on their terms, not ours. In an increasingly commoditized world, where there is little to differentiate our products and services, the real battleground for our customers' attention no longer revolves around what we do, it revolves around what matters to our customers.

This is what I mean by 'outside-in', a customer focus so relentless that no matter what we do, we continually ask ourselves: 'Does this matter to our customers?'

And nowhere is this more apparent than on social media, which I explore further in Chapter 10 in a discussion about becoming social businesses.

Who moved my cheese?

One of my favourite business books of all time is *Who Moved My Cheese: An amazing way to deal with change in your work and in your life*, by Dr Spencer Johnson (1998). It's a charming little story of four mice who live in a maze and look for cheese to sustain them and make them happy. The problem is that one day, unexpectedly, the cheese isn't where they've always found it.

Of course, cheese is a metaphor for what's important to us, what drives and nourishes us, in work and in life. The maze is where we look for that sustenance, and the story is a parable for how different people deal with change (Figure 1.4).

Figure 1.4 The handwriting on the wall

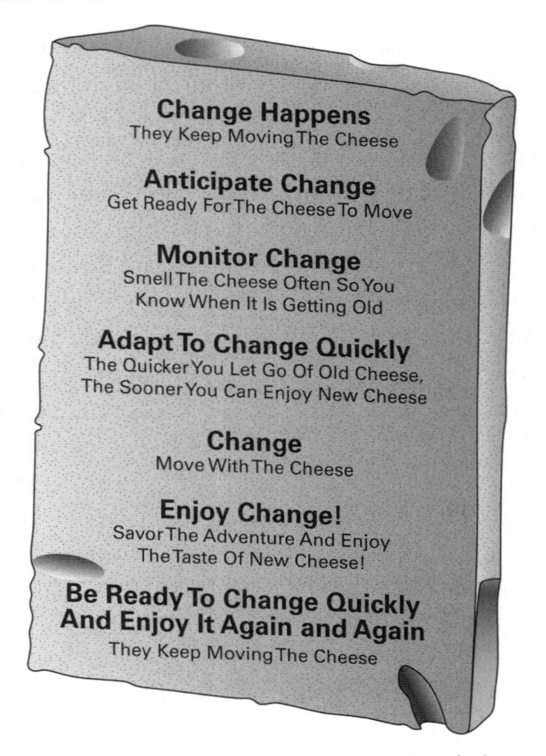

SOURCE Reprinted with permission from Dr Spencer Johnson, author of *Who Moved My Cheese?*

The cheese reminds us that while change may sometimes be difficult, it isn't inherently scary. Because change also brings opportunity and discovery, we just have to be open to finding it. In my own marketing career, there have been both decades of prosperity and years of stagnation, a dot-com boom and bust, the housing crisis and a global recession. I've worked in different industries and sectors, and had to continually reinvent myself as a marketer as new technologies changed the buyer landscape or enabled new routes to market, thus changing what I 'did' as a B2B marketer.

How are B2B marketers responding to change?

The times we live in are no different, except that the pace of change continues to increase exponentially.

Change: the economy goes down, comes back up and goes down yet again; a general election replaces one party with another; new technology means new skills to learn and new channels to explore; people leave and others join our organizations; there are restructures within our businesses – new bosses, new teams, new priorities, new focus.

We have no control over most of these things, which can be stressful, even though we can choose to consider them as opportunities to stimulate new and different behaviours, ways of working and outcomes. Still, I continue to see a reluctance from many B2B marketers to truly embrace change and think in different ways. The bulk of our B2B marketing effort continues to be done on features, benefits and price, even though we are operating in an increasingly commoditized world where there is very little differentiation between our products and services – bigger, better, faster, cheaper is no longer a compelling enough reason for our customers to buy from us.

We continue to do too much marketing 'stuff', in the same ways, year after year – albeit with new tools and through new channels – even in the midst of this undeniable change. As I've mentioned, we've had a particularly tough time getting to grips with social media in any meaningful way. We haven't yet completed (and many of us haven't even begun) the move towards thinking of ourselves as social businesses and the majority of us are still using all these new channels as push channels.

We must begin to understand that the old ways of working and the old measures of marketing 'success' are no longer relevant. The customer buying journey has fundamentally changed and we must change with it. This means thinking very differently about what we do, in very different ways.

Many of us are getting there. But along the way, too many of us have become completely focused on tactics and channels, with little or no alignment to our brand, our strategy (if we have one!) or our customers. We have become so obsessed with what we now need to do as marketers – all those new tactics, all these different outputs – we simply don't see that what we do may have changed, but how and why we do it has not. Our marketing discipline is founded on understanding our customers and then developing the marketing strategy that helps our organization win in the marketplace. All that follows is the tactical execution, which is certainly important, but it's not the most important part of our jobs.

Because marketing has not changed. Brand, strategy and customers remain the foundation for all marketing activity. This is not rocket science, it's Marketing 101, what all properly trained marketers should know and understand – no matter the business environment, no matter the technology. Yet there's clearly a disconnect between what we may know and what we may actually do.

Our headlong rush to embrace 'digital' and keep up with the rapid and constant change that threatens to overwhelm us has come at the expense of the core principles that should form the foundation for all of our marketing activity. Furthermore, too many of us are completely ignoring the so-called 'traditional' tactics and channels, which remain relevant to our customers, so should remain relevant to us. Our customers make no distinction between channels and neither should we. We absolutely need to stop and think about where our customers really are, despite the hype, and do a better job of integrating 'traditional' and 'digital'.

And this is the fallacy that we've been operating under for the past few years – that all this new technology, all these new tools, tactics and channels, has fundamentally changed the discipline of marketing. Thus we focus so exclusively on the tactical elements of marketing that they've become the only activity that matters for our B2B marketing functions.

All that glitters 02

B2B marketing's obsession with the latest tools and tactics

Every autumn we start to see a trickle of what becomes a new year's flood of marketing 'top trends' and 'predictions' for the year ahead. And every year the vast majority of this 'insight' is from a marketing 'inside-out' perspective, focused on the technologies, tools and tactics that are the 'must-haves' for marketers in the coming year. Of course, we all know how technology has fundamentally changed our customers' buying behaviours, profoundly altering how they engage with our organizations and thus impacting what we choose to do as marketers. And we need to know and understand what's here and what's on the horizon, as well what's driving the consumer world, because sooner or later these same consumers will be bringing these behaviours into the B2B world.

But we remain obsessed by these latest shiny new trends and quickly adopt their associated buzzwords, leaping into the new medium or format or channel as if this time it is going to solve all our B2B marketing woes. Yet there will always be something new that we will need to get to grips with during our long marketing careers. Technology will continue to transform our lives. Granted, the pace of that change just keeps on accelerating, until we feel like we are barely keeping up. But instead of getting sidetracked by all these shiny new things, shouldn't we focus on the new thinking that is necessary to address the incredibly big challenges our businesses and our customers are and will be facing, outside-in?

Because even though B2B marketing continues to make a lot of headway into this digitally driven, social era, we are still placing too much emphasis on what marketing does – the tasks and outputs – instead of what our customers and businesses want and need. What if we stopped for a moment and thought a little bit more about the marketing outcomes we want to achieve, instead of all these cool new tools and technologies that may or may not be the right ones for us?

If we can get this part right first, perhaps we'll move much further towards making our marketing efforts and thus our businesses more meaningful and memorable to our customers.

'Marketing myopia'

In 1960, Harvard Business School marketing professor Theodore Levitt published a paper in the *Harvard Business Review* where he coined the term 'marketing myopia' – a near-sighted focus on selling products and services, rather than seeing the big picture of what customers really want. When the *Harvard Business Review* reprinted the article in 2004, it described marketing myopia as the most influential marketing idea of the past half-century.

In the article, Levitt encouraged business leaders to move from a short-sighted product-oriented mindset to a customer-oriented one and to answer a fundamental question: *what business are we in?* – his main thesis being that a business is defined not by the selling of a product but by fulfilling a customer need. Perhaps the most widely used example from his article is that of the railroad industry. Levitt argues that the railroads fell into steep decline because they thought they were in the train business – selling passenger journeys – rather than the transportation business. If they had thought differently about their business, about moving goods and people from one place to another, they might have done differently, by diversifying their business into other forms of transportation such as cars, trucks or aeroplanes.

More than 50 years later, in August 2016, Amy Gallo wrote 'A refresher on marketing myopia' in the *Harvard Business Review*, exploring its application to business and marketers in the 21st century. In the article, Gallo speaks to John Deighton, a professor at Harvard Business School and an authority on consumer behaviour and marketing, about the continuing relevance of marketing myopia in the current business environment.

Deighton maintains that it's extremely easy for marketers themselves to become myopic about what they do – they get so caught up in developing marketing plans and programmes, delivering campaigns and executing tactics that they lose sight of the bigger picture, rarely stopping long enough to ask or answer the question, why are we doing what we are doing?

In Gallo's article, Deighton reinforces the concept of marketing myopia as still relevant, 'in part because the original idea wasn't very prescriptive. Levitt didn't offer "ten steps to eliminate marketing myopia". Instead, he was all about provoking people to think differently.'

Deighton also believes that Levitt's article is still so significant because it reminds CEOs that marketing is part of their job: '[Levitt] tells the leader of the organization: you are in business because you have a customer. Therefore, you have to think about marketing' (Deighton in Gallo, 2016).

And he is quick to warn that 'technology, social media, and other advances are changing the way companies market themselves... But let's not forget, even as we admire the shiniest and newest ideas, that some approaches, like "marketing myopia", have lasted for a long time and are likely to do so for a long time still.'

While both Levitt's and Deighton's emphasis is centred on the consumer world, this is a stark reminder for B2B marketers – not all that glitters will bring in the gold.

The 'new' marketing myopia

Over the past half-century, consumer marketers have indeed heeded Levitt's advice by focusing on customers. However, in 2010, Craig Smith, Minette E Drumwright and Mary C Gentile – in their article 'The new marketing myopia' in the *Journal of Public Policy & Marketing* – suggested that the pendulum had swung too far, that with their relentless focus on the customer, marketers were failing to see the broader societal context that influences decision-making. They make the case that:

> Marketers suffering from the new marketing myopia view the customer only as a 'consumer'... The customer is not viewed as a citizen, a parent, an employee, a community member, or a member of a global village with a long-term stake in the future of the planet. (Smith et al, 2010, 4–11)

They argued that organizations need to understand that 'consumption' involves a wider set of stakeholders who are concerned about a company's social and environmental impacts – and that these stakeholders may also include the company's customers.

B2B marketing myopia

The development of the marketing myopia concept to include the broader societal influences of the buying process is especially important in B2B, where there is little that differentiates us from our competitors. As I've mentioned previously, in an increasingly commoditized world, our customers don't just buy what we do or how we do it, they buy why we do it. They buy products and services that improve both their businesses and their own lives, but they also want to do business with companies who contribute to the greater good. This is the real battleground for our customers' attention – it no longer revolves around what we do, it revolves around what matters to our customers. In Chapter 5 I look more closely at the customer imperative because B2B hasn't yet fully embraced a customer-first perspective. As I described in the example of the lost pitch in the previous chapter, we tend to become obsessed with what we know and do, to the detriment of the wider business.

Short-sightedness is not limited to marketers. When people are uncertain about the future, it's a natural human tendency for people to focus on what they know. But I would argue that it's precisely in times of uncertainty that we need to expand our thinking, not narrow it.

Yet the organizations we work for in B2B – and especially professional services – continue to be highly risk averse. In addition, they've historically been relationship driven, with sales 'owning' those relationships. Both these factors have led us as B2B marketers to being less concerned with the customer than with our own, often limited, tasks. We continue to do what we've always done because it has always (more or less) worked.

This is a risky approach for marketers. When the economy is good and our businesses are growing with relative ease, 'good enough' tends to be good enough. But ever since the global economic crisis of 2008, we have come under increasing pressure to justify our marketing efforts.

As this pressure mounts to 'prove' marketing value within our B2B organizations, many of us – for the very first time – actually have to develop proper marketing plans. In later chapters I discuss the error we make when we develop marketing plans without a marketing strategy. But most often this isn't actually our fault. It's what's asked of us by our marketing leadership, who have not fulfilled their responsibility to develop the marketing strategy for the organization. The marketing plan thus too often becomes regarded as a chore, imposed upon us from above. And we go through the motions because it's required of us in order to secure our annual budgets. In fact, time and again I see marketers start the planning process with the budget – this is how much I'm going to ask for, based on what I had last year – and then back-filling with the tactics that use up this budget!

Because we are good at the tactics. And again, it's not really our fault, it's what our leadership asks of us. Most of us are measured, promoted and receive pay rises based on our ability to deliver the plan. And although we may be committed to our organization's success, we are all disproportionately interested in our own success. Again, there's nothing wrong with this;

we all want to succeed. But it becomes an issue that impacts our effectiveness if we 'follow the herd', simply because it may be interpreted as out of touch with the 'latest and greatest' marketing.

Our focus on tactics thus becomes a default straight to delivery and completely omits the critical thinking that's necessary to really make a difference to our businesses.

Traditional versus new (digital) marketing

We are now marketing in a digital world. Digital has become such a pervasive part of our lives that perhaps we can forgive the less experienced marketers among us who think this means we do 'digital marketing'. But it isn't just the least experienced among us who now proclaim that traditional marketing is broken, obsolete, dead. Wide debate continues as to whether digital marketing is taking over traditional marketing. Many marketers even believe that traditional marketing barely exists any more, if at all.

So, what do we mean by the terms 'traditional' and 'digital'?

Digital marketing is used as an all-encompassing term for the marketing of products or services through the use of digital technologies. These technologies are most often associated with the internet, yet the term 'digital' also refers to marketing through devices such as mobile phones, and channels such as online advertising, e-mail and social media.

Everything else that might be in a marketer's toolkit is considered 'traditional'. This includes: television, radio and print advertising; outdoor display; trade shows, conferences and other face-to-face customer events; direct mail; print and promotional materials.

But this is where it gets confusing; for example, digital technology is now used for hard copy printing and outdoor display, and e-mail – though a digital medium – is often considered as 'traditional' as direct mail through the postal service. The lines between traditional and digital marketing are becoming ever more indistinguishable.

'Digital' was originally a subset of marketing in B2B, and rightly so. New tools and new channels needed new skills and expertise. And many may remember the days when our websites were an afterthought to other marketing activity. But digital now oozes throughout every aspect of marketing. It has become simply yet another, albeit important, instrument in our toolkit. So, at least in the context of marketing, isn't the use of the term 'digital' now redundant?

As I mentioned in Chapter 1, digital has, in effect, become invisible, like electricity, powering our world, taken for granted. We must stop worrying about where digital ends and so-called 'traditional' marketing begins. Our customers certainly don't differentiate between traditional and digital marketing channels, so why should we? It's all marketing.

Yet there is a danger that B2B marketers still latch on to solely digital tactics and channels because they are comparatively easier to measure than traditional marketing tactics and channels. There are all sorts of metrics for views, shares, clicks, downloads, likes, open rates and so on that marketers use in their ongoing drive to prove marketing ROI for their organizations. I explore ROI in B2B further in Chapter 5, but easier does not necessarily mean better. Marketers who treat 'digital' as separate to the traditional marketing mix will ultimately find themselves less successful than others who use an integrated mix of traditional and digital in support of their organization's strategy and targets.

It's crucial to look at digital within the context of the entire marketing strategy. Digital versus traditional is not an either/or choice. It all comes back to the customer journey and creating a seamless experience no matter where our customers are in that journey. Fully integrating what has been a distinct discipline is a necessity that reflects our customers' current buying behaviours.

Mark Ritson is a professor of marketing who has taught at the London Business School, the Melbourne Business School, Singapore Management University and MIT Sloan School of Management. He also regularly writes in marketing publications and, in the UK, is the outspoken back-page columnist for *Marketing Week* magazine. Mark has further argued that the divide between digital and traditional 'is artificial and unhelpful' and has stopped marketers from looking at the big picture. His argument is that marketers forget that it's 'digital that provides the execution and is fundamentally tactical. Great marketing starts with the objectives and only then [should marketers] adopt the tools and channels that best lead to those outcomes' (Ritson, 2016). Not vice versa. I totally agree with Mark that this creation of the 'Digital Marketer' all but ensures that the channel will be selected first and then the justification for that choice built into it after the fact. How does that make sense?

Furthermore, we need to remember that no matter the hype, all the research of the past few years continues to illustrate that the so-called traditional marketing tactics of both the B2C and B2B worlds remain the most effective.

Contrary to what we've been led to believe by so many marketing pundits, television remains the dominant medium of our time. Adobe does a large, ongoing piece of research called The Adobe Digital Index. In their June 2016 report, they found that television is growing – by 107 per cent year-on-year. While TV is generally a very small portion of B2B marketing, this should be a wake-up call that makes us question many of the so-called truths we are being told about digital.

Some statistics from a range of researchers (Michael Brenner, 2016) reveal the paradox for B2B marketers:

- The most effective marketing tactic (75 per cent) for B2B businesses is in-person events (Content Marketing Institute, 2016 Benchmarking Report).
- 74 per cent of respondents said they would increase spend on events in the coming year (Regalix, State of B2B Marketing Report, 2016).
- Website (86 per cent) and e-mail (72 per cent) lead the pack of online channels (Regalix, State of B2B Marketing Report, 2016).
- E-mail and websites are not only the most effective tactics used, they are also two of the least difficult tactics to execute (Ascend2, 2016).
- 75 per cent of marketers still send their content marketing directly via e-mail (ALF Insight, 2016).
- Over half (56 per cent) of companies agree that e-mail offers 'excellent' to 'good' ROI (Econsultancy, 2016).
- Measuring the revenue impact from digital marketing spend remains the toughest challenge for B2B marketers (DemandWave, 2016).

Face-to-face and e-mail – the first a 'traditional' marketing tactic and the second a traditional tactic (direct mail) via a digital channel – remain the most effective and most used tools for B2B marketers.

Given that digital is often assumed to be easier to measure than traditional marketing activity, it's even more telling that measurement remains such a tough challenge for B2B marketers (I explore the ROI challenge further in Chapter 5).

Sir Martin Sorrell has stated that 'Brands are starting to question if they have over-invested in digital' (Vizard, 2016). And while he is clearly speaking in the context of B2C, we in B2B would do well to take heed.

A 2015 study conducted by neuromarketing research company TrueImpact for the *Canada Post* looked at the brain's response to different marketing tactics and channels. Using brain imaging and eye-tracking technology to 'see' into the brains of people interacting with traditional (direct mail) and digital (e-mail, display) media, they found traditional tactics were more effective than the digital equivalents.

Their white paper – *A Bias for Action* – explores four key findings:

- Direct mail is easier to understand and more memorable than digital media. It takes 21 per cent less thought to process and creates a much higher brand recall.
- Direct mail is far more persuasive than digital media. Its motivation response is 20 per cent higher – and even better if it appeals to senses beyond touch, such as smell and hearing.
- Direct mail gets the message across faster. Our brains process it quicker than digital media.
- Direct mail is more likely to drive consumers to act on the message than digital media.

While this study was conducted in the context of consumers and their responses to specific retail channels, it underlines an important point. If our B2B customers are bringing their consumer buying behaviours into the B2B world, these neurological responses will be the same or extremely similar in a B2B environment, further underscoring the importance of integrating our online and offline channels.

May I have your attention, please?

We've all heard that thanks to technology – mobile technology in particular – our attention span has fallen to 8.25 seconds, less than that of a goldfish, which is thought to be 9 seconds. There even appears to be some science to prove it. But is this another truism that we've taken on board without challenge?

Are we marketing to goldfish? This widely quoted goldfish statistic actually originates from a 2015 Microsoft report entitled 'How does digital affect Canadian attention spans?'. In the survey, 2000 Canadian participants were asked about their use of mobile technology, websites and online games. Yet, according to Jonathan Schwabish – founder of PolicyViz and a senior researcher at the Urban Institute, a non-profit research institution in Washington DC – attention span was not even tested as part of the study! Furthermore, he was not able to verify two key sources cited in the study.

In a 2015 *Telegraph* article, 'Humans have shorter attention span than goldfish, thanks to smartphones', Bruce Morton, a researcher with the University of Western Ontario's Brain and Mind Institute, explained that humans crave information: 'Just because we may be allocating our attention differently as a function of the technologies we may be using, it doesn't mean that the way our attention actually functions has changed.'

Yet the media and many B2B marketers would have us believe that people – and our customers – no longer have any capacity to concentrate. In fact, an online search for 'attention span of a goldfish' yielded 262,000 results, the first page of which contained articles from *Time* magazine, *The New York Times*, *The Telegraph* and *The Independent*, among others, including an article and infographic titled 'How to market to goldfish'.

The myth of the shrinking attention span

As marketers, we've been told for years that we need to create 'bite-size' content that's quickly and easily digestible and shareable in order to capture our customers' attention effectively. We continue to be told by the marketing experts that size matters and shorter is better – for example, our blogs should be a maximum of 500 words and our video three minutes or less.

Yet still we sit and watch a film for two to three hours; still we spend hours reading our favourite novels. We've even begun to hear more and more about 'long-form content' on the internet, content that is 2,000 or more words in length. There is increasing evidence that long-form content not only gets read, but also ranks better in search engines and converts better than short-form content.

> Our attention spans aren't shrinking, there is just so much less that actually compels our attention.

Think about the great novels, the gorgeous writing that keeps us captivated and immersed in the story, every word, thought and idea driving us towards the next. Or the great films that hook us into the story right from the start, keeping us glued to the screen until the credits roll, on the edge of our seats, compelled to see what happens next.

As humans, we crave ever more information, emotion, ideas, insight or entertainment – and 8.25 seconds' worth of content doesn't come close to satisfying that craving. We don't care how long a book or an article or a video is, as long as we have a compelling reason to pay attention. Yet there is simply way too much content out there that is consistently mediocre or completely boring. No wonder we don't pay attention to most of it!

We must stop equating human attention span to that of a goldfish; it's a fiction which only serves as an excuse for marketers to continue creating content that is not grabbing anyone's attention. We have to start giving our customers reasons to pay attention. And length doesn't matter at all.

The power of words – making marketing up close and personal

Which brings me to the power of words. The language we use impacts the ways in which we think and behave. Whether written, verbal or visual, language is how we communicate and influence. It's how we tell our stories, and the best stories – and the best marketing – resonate on a very personal and emotional level. Writers, orators and film-makers innately understand this, yet marketers don't think or do enough about it. Words shape every form of communication we may utilize as marketers. Even if we're creating a video, we start with a written script. Yet many of us are mediocre, even poor, writers.

Words have the power to create a personal and emotional connection with our customers. I discussed emotions in B2B marketing in Chapter 1 and we need to remember that emotion runs throughout our customer engagement. Without emotion, there can be no attention or impact. Our customers are people, not job titles; we don't market or sell to faceless organizations (or goldfish), but to very real people who just happen to be at work.

A few years ago there was a powerful video making the rounds on social networks that was titled *The Power of Words*. It was produced by an agency selling its creative services and many were moved to tears the first time they saw it:

A beggar sits on a busy high street with a cardboard sign that says: 'I'm blind. Please help.' A few people are dropping their pocket change in front of him, but most passers-by are ignoring him. Until a young woman walks by, stops, turns around and stands in front of him. He touches her shoes, which are textured leather lace-up short boots. She looks at him and looks at the sign, pulls a marking pen out of her handbag, picks up the sign, writes something on it, and walks off – probably to her job as a marketer!

All through the rest of that day, the high street gets busier and busier, and everyone is giving the beggar spare change, until he has a huge pile of coins in front of and all around him. Eventually the young marketing woman returns – probably on her way home from work – and stands in front of him again. He recognizes her by her boots and asks her: 'What did you do to my sign?' She replies: 'Same thing, different words.' Cue the mood music and the camera pans from the beggar to the sign, which now reads: 'It's a beautiful day and I can't see it.'

Even years later, this video remains in the memory, because this kind of emotional impact is not just for consumer marketing. It's a potent reminder of the power of emotion in customer engagement, how making something personal can create an impact that makes a difference. This is the power of words and this is what we should be aspiring to in B2B marketing – creating an emotive frame of reference that our customers can personally relate to.

Magpie mania: where should we focus our marketing?

But we B2B marketers are magpies. We are drawn to the brightest and shiniest new things. Every new trend becomes the latest must-have in order to *really* be great B2B marketers. And just like each year's must-have Christmas toy or fashion accessory, we ignore everything else in our toy box or wardrobe until we've completely worn it out and moved on to the next. Because we have bought into the fallacy that marketing has changed so dramatically that if we are not doing these things then we are not very good marketers.

In our continuing quest to, above all else, be *valued* within our organizations, we also love words, phrases and activities that sound important and weighty. If the last greatest best marketing preoccupation didn't work, then we simply call it something else, without actually thinking about it any differently, or we quickly move on to the next.

But this is just a symptom of the bigger challenge – marketing's almost complete focus on tools and channels. Practically every discussion I have about marketing ends up being a discussion about tactics instead of strategy.

And we all should know by now that without strategy, tactics are just more 'stuff' in an already overcrowded world.

So, where should we focus our marketing attention?

Storytelling remains the beating heart of marketing

As human beings, we are drawn to, connect with and remember stories. We are simply not able to remember dry facts and data for very long. But we feel stories. In fact, storytelling in marketing is really nothing new; the best marketing and advertising activities have used storytelling to great effect since long before the digital and social era. Good stories are timeless. They surprise us, entertain us, make us think, and most importantly they make us feel. And what we feel is memorable, staying with us long after the story ends.

Storytelling was all the rage among B2B marketers not that long ago. Stories would make us more human and connect us more closely to our customers; marketing through storytelling would build and maintain those emotional connections in a way that facts and logic could not.

Yet we don't hear much about storytelling in B2B marketing any more and it's because as B2B organizations we struggle to articulate any story beyond what we sell. So, storytelling has become 'too difficult' for many of us. And as marketers, we become so consumed with what our companies do at a functional level that we continue to use the bland and stale words, phrases and acronyms that may be meaningful to us, but completely lack a narrative to stimulate the mind and the emotions of our customers.

Everything we do as marketers tells a story, whether we intend to or not. We need to start thinking differently about these narratives and work harder at developing ongoing, interlinking stories that align to our customers. We must stop talking about ourselves and start thinking like our customers, with a focus on them, and tell the stories that are meaningful to them, that they can connect with emotionally. By providing the thread that joins up all our marketing activity, these stories have the power to deliver impact and differentiation in the hearts and minds of our customers, and by doing so make our organizations truly memorable.

Content marketing is failing us

An entire new industry has sprung up around 'content marketing', creating a totally separate discipline within our profession. There are scores of content marketing agencies and completely new content marketing roles; there's even an Institute and a massively attended annual conference, all focused on content marketing.

We've been told that content marketing is an historic transformation for companies and marketers everywhere. That our companies and our marketing functions need to act more like publishers, in the process hiring journalists to create the kind of content necessary to stand out in this era of information (read content) overload.

But, while it's great that journalists and other writers are reinventing themselves for the corporate world, and that there's new attention on the content we produce and push out into the marketplace, many of us are missing the point. Contrary to what we've been told, there is no such thing as content marketing. It's one part of the marketing mix, a tactic, and it's what marketing has always done, albeit through new channels and a renewed customer perspective.

The Content Marketing Institute defines content marketing as 'a strategic marketing approach focused on creating and distributing valuable, relevant, and consistent content to attract and retain a clearly defined audience – and, ultimately, to drive profitable customer action'. Yet, this definition could apply to every aspect of the marketing mix. Furthermore, content can only be strategic if there is an overall marketing strategy with which that content is aligned.

Because marketing is impossible without content. Content is what we use to engage with our customers – whether it's written, verbal, auditory or visual. And regardless of the marketing tactics or channels, content is a part of every element of the marketing mix.

In Part Two, I use the Coca-Cola Content 2020 Initiative as an example of 'doing different' in our social era. It's been held up by many 'content marketers' as an illustration of 'content marketing' that works. Yet Coca-Cola never uses the term, instead highlighting how content is integral to all marketing activity by emphasizing content as the means through which customers understand and engage with brands.

What we need to remember is that 'content marketing' has simply emerged in response to the fundamental changes in the customer buying journey. In essence, 'content marketing' is intended to shift our marketing focus away from what we sell to what's important to our customers – in other words, engaging with our customers on their terms, from their perspective, not ours.

But 'content marketing' is ultimately failing us. Even the Content Marketing Institute, in its 2017 B2B Content Marketing Benchmarking Reports for the United States, UK and Australia, found that one-third or less of B2B marketers say they are successful or effective at content marketing (34 per cent in the United States and 25 per cent for both the UK and Australia). Furthermore, 70–79 per cent of these same marketers will produce more content next year even though almost two-thirds don't have a real understanding of what content is effective and what isn't.

Content marketing has become almost solely about the *creation* of content. But instead of asking ourselves what kind of content we want to create, shouldn't we first be asking ourselves what kind of engagement with our customers we want to have? Like the overdependence upon 'digital' as a descriptor for marketing, a focus on content marketing implies a tactical choice before understanding what we are trying to achieve, for both our brands and our customers.

Despite our obsession with it, 'content marketing' is distracting us from our real job as marketers, which is about engaging with our customers. We have become so focused on producing content that we've forgotten to do the actual marketing of it. And this is worrying, that we are treating 'content marketing' as if it is something separate to what we do as marketers.

Digital and social media marketing

I'd like to delete every word I see that precedes 'marketing'. It's all marketing.

I have discussed 'digital marketing' earlier in this chapter but the term and its current use bear another look. Way back in 2013, Marc Pritchard, Chief Brand Officer at Procter & Gamble, declared that 'Digital is Dead' in his keynote address at Dmexco (Digital Marketing Exhibition and Conference). In that speech, he warned that digital marketing is simply a tool for engagement, an important tool, but just one component of the marketing mix.

Yet, even though we should be looking at consumer marketing for guidance, all these years later B2B marketing remains preoccupied with digital, even when other, more traditional, channels prove more effective. And what exactly do we mean by 'digital' in B2B? If the structure of our marketing departments provides any clues, then 'digital' is actually synonymous with our websites and thus in practice translates to how we drive inbound traffic to our website.

The main reason for such a focus comes down to ROI. For the first time we have the ability to specifically measure – and thus justify – B2B marketing activity. We now have the tools to measure not only the number of people who come to our website, but who they are and what 'digital assets' they 'consume'. These metrics are helping us to deliver better-quality leads to our sales teams. I discuss ROI and metrics in depth at the end of Chapter 4, but focusing on a single channel is risky for B2B marketers. It presumes the same customer behaviour in all situations without bearing in mind that our customers move seamlessly between online and offline.

A subset of this thinking is that around 'social media marketing', another tactic that's driven through a digital channel. Make no mistake, social media is not a strategy, just as digital is not a strategy. I explore strategy and tactics in detail in Part Two, but for now it's critical to understand that while both are an integral part of the marketing plan, they are not the starting point. And by creating these '[fill in the blank] marketing' silos we are in real danger of eliminating marketing strategy from our profession.

As Mark Ritson (2016) said, 'You can't be a good marketer if you've started with a tool. Start with the customer and the strategy and then choose the tools.'

From 'Big Data' to analytics

Do you remember when 'Big Data' burst onto the B2B marketing scene? In 2013 it was the headline topic at seemingly every marketing conference. SAS describes the term as 'the ever-increasing volume, velocity, variety, variability and complexity of information' – both structured and unstructured – that inundates us every day. But while the term 'Big Data' is relatively new, the actual act of gathering and analysing the information available to us has long been a part of marketing. Data simply became big when technology enabled us to access and gather a whole lot more of it in new ways. However, it's not the amount of data that's important. It's the quality of the data and how we as marketers interpret it that matters, and then what we do with it to inform and support our strategy and business decisions.

Data analytics is the latest manifestation of the data explosion, the realization that all this data can be used to better understand and even predict customer behaviour. It has the potential to help us to learn, to recognize what we don't know, and to craft more relevant customer engagement.

But like everything 'new' with marketing, there are challenges. Are we using data to provide actual insight or to validate what we think we already know? Data providers and data analysts are not strategic advisers and in B2B we tend to skew our data to fit *what we think we know* about our customers. Furthermore, an overly reliant focus on data tends to shift the marketing attention towards what we've already done instead of what we should be doing next.

Marketing has always tried to predict customer behaviour, and predictive analytics provides us with new tools. But the challenge remains: predictive analytics assumes that past behaviour forecasts future behaviour, even though we have learned that this is simply not so.

There is ongoing debate about whether marketing is art or science, and I explore this further at the end of Chapter 7. Although, in fact, marketing needs to be both, we mustn't ever forget that we are emotional beings and emotional buyers, even in B2B. And data will never fully describe or predict the behaviours of our customers.

Personas are not real people

How, then, can we ever know and understand our customers?

The development of 'buyer personas' remains a staple offering for many of the external marketing agencies we might employ. And many of us have gone through this process, either with an agency or with our teams. In many cases, creating buyer personas has been an important first step in beginning to think from a customer perspective.

What exactly is a persona? According to Hubspot, 'Personas are fictional, generalized characters that encompass the various needs, goals, and observed behavior patterns among your real and potential customers' (November 2016), and they provide guidance on best practice for creating personas using their tools.

A buyer persona is intended to describe a group of customers with:

- demographic and biographical information;
- common behaviour patterns;
- shared professional and personal 'issues';
- general professional and personal goals and wishes.

These personas may be based on real people, but critically, *they are not real people*. Understanding our customers goes much, much deeper than a one-page buyer persona. Yet many of us never go beyond these personas when we develop our marketing strategy or our marketing plans.

We talk a lot about understanding our customers in B2B, and in Chapter 1 I talked about how language influences our thinking about our customers. In the same manner, if we don't develop a fuller sense for who our customers really are, we are doomed to perpetuate less effective marketing.

We have started to realize that we must step out from our organizational marketing silo and connect more effectively with our sales teams. But most of us still don't interact with our sales teams on a regular basis. In fact, many marketing teams don't even sit within the same building as their sales teams. And, more importantly, how many of us ever actually have a direct conversation with a customer?

Only by regularly interacting with our salespeople and speaking directly to our customers can we ever get the real customer insight we crave.

Personalization or Personal – what's the difference?

Technology and marketing automation has enabled a more personalized approach to consumer marketing online – witness the Amazon 'suggestions' that follow us around the site when we shop. And many other consumer brands have utilized personalization to great effect – Coca-Cola's 'Share a Coke' campaign may be among the most well-known examples.

The theory is that it's more effective than mass marketing or targeted marketing – both one-to-many approaches – through one-to-one marketing.

But is it? Even with all this technology available to us, do our B2B customers even want one-to-one marketing? Or are we confusing what we actually mean by and intend with 'personalization'? Isn't our real challenge in B2B about making marketing personal to our customers?

I tend to speak a lot about how language impacts the ways in which we think and behave. So, as I've done before, I looked up the definitions in the dictionary:

- **Personalize** means *to design or produce (something) to meet someone's individual requirements*; its synonyms are 'customize' and 'individualize'.
- On the other hand, **Personal** means *of or concerning one's emotions*; its synonyms are 'intimate' and 'subjective'.

That's a fundamental difference in meaning. And a fundamental difference in what we choose to do as marketers. Because in B2B we seem to just be waking up to the fact that the best marketing is personal. And to get personal, we need to stop talking about what we sell. We need to stop talking about our products and services and start focusing on what's important to our customers.

Customer experience is the new customer centricity

As if we don't already have enough to distract us, the latest bandwagon to roll through our B2B marketing universe is customer experience (CX). Driven by the attention that CX is garnering in the B2C marketing world, B2B marketers are enthusiastically signing up to 'own' CX within our organizations.

The *Harvard Business Review* defines customer experience as 'the sum totality of how customers engage with your company and brand, not just as a snapshot in time, but throughout the entire arc of being a customer' (28 October 2010). These are all the interactions – the cumulative experiences across multiple touchpoints through multiple channels over time – taken together as a whole – from initial awareness of an organization's products or services, through the buyer journey to purchase, and beyond to include the user journey.

In its 2016 report sponsored by Marketo, 'The path to 2020: marketers seize the customer experience', the Economist Intelligence Unit (EIU) found that 86 per cent of marketers say they will own the end-to-end customer experience by 2020. The survey further found that CMOs for consumer brands are most focused on the data and analytics that enable them to 'personalize the end-to-end customer experience across platforms, locations and physical objects'.

Another research report, 'CXcellence: how to achieve CX success in B2B 2016–17', by B2B Marketing in association with Circle Research, found that 70 per cent of B2B marketers say that creating an excellent customer experience is a top priority and fully 84 per cent say they'll be placing more emphasis on CX over the next 12 months.

But isn't CX just another way of talking about the integration of marketing tactics across all marketing channels to ensure that this activity in its entirety is focused on the customer? Is it presuming the trend towards greater personalization for B2B? Furthermore, has anyone actually asked the question whether the user journey *should* fall within marketing?

In practice in B2B marketing, the focus appears to be predominantly on the customer satisfaction portion of CX. Customer satisfaction has historically fallen under the domain of customer service teams. Yet, according to the Salesforce 2016 State of Marketing research, for the second year running, customer satisfaction is the number one success metric for marketers across both B2C and B2B organizations today.

B2B marketing is eager to take on this responsibility for customer satisfaction and include it under the banner of customer experience. Customer satisfaction – whether positive or negative – is, after all, the natural outcome of the 'sum totality' of how our customers feel about every aspect of engagement with our organizations. Of particular relevance to marketing, customer satisfaction is not only measurable, but our C-suite understands and highly values these metrics. So, in our continuing quest to 'prove' marketing value within our B2B organizations, we want to 'own' this and thus every part of the customer experience.

But should we? Is CX merely another example of marketing focusing on the wrong things? Because there are two elements in the 'sum totality' of CX that no one's talking about: first, the role that marketing must play in engaging the customer before their buyer journey even begins; and second, the continuing engagement that marketing should have with the customer once they are a user, engagement that contributes to customer satisfaction but is not about customer satisfaction.

What exactly is the role and purpose of marketing? I explore this theme in depth in Part Three.

Thinking different about B2B marketing

03

CASE STUDY Apple's iconic 'Think Different' campaign

It's hard to believe, but 20 years ago, in 1997, Apple was in real trouble. They had a tiny portion of the market (around 2 per cent), $2 billion of year-on-year losses, and hardly any software applications in comparison to Windows PCs.

Sure, there was a core group of Apple fanatics, almost solely in the creative industries, and they had a solid education and home computing business. But the broader business world thought Apple computers were not capable of 'real' computing. And the industry press thought Apple computers were 'toys', constantly implying that for the general public to buy an Apple product would be the height of stupidity.

A large proportion of the world thought Apple was going to die.

Fast-forward to 2011 and Apple was ranked the most valuable company in the world. And further forward to 2015, when the B2B company I was with moved everyone in the UK firm (some 9,000+ people) to iPhones for their business phone. In 1997, if you had told any business that they would be using an Apple product for their day-to-day business needs, you would have been laughed out of the room. Who could have imagined that Apple would become a mainstream business purchase?

So, what changed? In 1997, Steve Jobs returned to Apple as their interim CEO, a decade after he had left the company he founded, and he quickly made some key changes:

- First, he reduced Apple's product line from 14 down to 4.
- Second, he consolidated all of the company's advertising worldwide into one new agency. For context, when he came back to Apple, the company was

running approximately 25 different advertising campaigns across the globe, all of which were independent campaigns focused on Apple's specific products and technology.

- Third, and critically, he knew that he had to do something about both industry and public perception of the Apple brand and its products.

And the iconic 'Think Different' campaign was born.

This campaign was really bold thinking for a small computer company in trouble. First, the concept itself was different. For those who remember, the television ad was shot solely in black and white, with a voice-over that did not once refer to the Apple brand or its products.

Most of the print ads consisted of just a single person – a few were of two people – also photographed in black and white, with simply the text 'Think Different', the multi-coloured Apple logo and the website address. Again, there was no product in the ads at all.

Interestingly, the ads didn't even identify the person in the photograph, and although many are instantly recognizable to the general public, like Muhammad Ali and Einstein, many are not, like Martha Graham, Frank Lloyd Wright and Jane Goodall – so that the images in a way became every man and every woman.

The execution was bold as well. This campaign did not run in a single computer or trade industry publication. Instead, Apple placed its ads on the back covers of magazines such as *BusinessWeek*, *Time*, *Newsweek* and the *New Yorker* in the United States, and brazenly used huge outdoor billboards, bus wraps and wall coverings.

Many didn't react positively at first and there was a lot of ridicule from both the media and the market. But the important point was that people were talking – and talking a lot – about a brand that had been almost completely dismissed by the market.

When the 'Think Different' campaign launched, Apple didn't even have any significant new products, yet they immediately felt the impact. Apple's stock price tripled in a year. A year after that, Apple introduced a computer design revolution with their multi-coloured iMacs. And the rest is history.

What B2B marketers can learn from Apple

I've always believed that we in B2B marketing can and should learn from the B2C world. And for me, the Apple story remains a compelling one. Even though our businesses may not be in the same kind of trouble as Apple was in 1997, and even though an awful lot has changed in the past 20 years, the fundamentals of marketing have remained the same and what Apple did in 1997 provides us with a masterclass in the three fundamentals of marketing: Brand, Strategy and Customers.

Lesson 1: Brand

Let's look first at the Apple brand.

Jobs talked about Apple's branding as addressing the question of 'What are we here to do?' In today's language, this was all about Apple's brand purpose. And asking this question led to a clear articulation of the Apple brand and what it stood for.

As Jobs told *The Wall Street Journal Europe* in April 1998: '"Think Different" celebrates the soul of the Apple brand – that creative people with passion can change the world.' Not only that; in essence, this campaign redefined the notion of 'creative' – by taking it out of the realm of the artsy and applying it to business, to science, to everyday achievement.

Lesson 2: Strategy

This clear articulation of Apple's brand purpose then led to a major change in their strategic direction. They stopped thinking and acting like a computer company and started acting like a company dedicated to creative thinking – no matter what industry or business their customer was in.

For me, this was the real power of their strategy: making what they do relevant and inspiring for those outside their former niche markets.

Lesson 3: Customers

But Apple's real genius was connecting their brand and strategy to their customers on an emotional level, to how people feel. Does this sound familiar? It should. Emotions in marketing have been a hot topic over the past few years in B2B marketing circles.

Apple thought and talked about their customers as creative people who inspire change. In the language of our times, these are the innovators, the disruptors, the entrepreneurs, the growth hackers. But Apple also tapped into the very real human aspiration of ordinary people for making a difference, whether that be in large ways or small.

And it clearly reached right in and touched the hearts and souls of people across all walks of life. Because it spoke to hopes and dreams, to the aspirations of people just like you and me. I can still remember seeing the 'Think Different' billboards for the first time on the roundabout driving onto the M4 from Heathrow in the UK. It was larger than life, it was powerful, it made me go 'Wow' and it made me THINK.

In Part One I have explored the environment in which we as B2B marketers are now working, one that insists we think differently about our customers, our organizations and our profession. I've looked at what's changed and what hasn't – including the buyer journey, the sales funnel, how we engage with our customers and how our customers engage with us, the language we use and the technology – and delved into some common misconceptions and assumptions that we have accepted without challenge, such as the assumed divide between traditional and digital marketing, and the supposed shrinking of our attention spans. I've considered the original 'marketing myopia' model and in the context of the 21st-century 'new marketing myopia', then expanded this thinking into what marketing myopia looks like in B2B marketing today. I've reviewed many of the influences that continue to occupy our thinking – including the tactics and the channels – and suggested the shift we need to make in our ingrained perceptions about marketing. Finally, I've looked at some of the areas where we should and shouldn't be focusing our attention as marketers in B2B.

In particular, I have put the spotlight once and for all on the fundamental marketing fallacy of our era – that our marketing discipline has changed beyond recognition – which is severely impacting our ability to think beyond our marketing silos and be effective marketers. We have become so busy getting to grips with all the new tactical elements and distribution channels for our marketing activity that they've become the only activity that matters for our B2B marketing functions.

The biggest risk we face as B2B marketers is that our marketing activity is not valued by our organizations. We continue to be viewed by our organizations as a cost instead of a driver for the business, a 'nice-to-have' instead of an integral component of achieving business strategy and objectives. B2B organizations – and especially professional services – have been slow to adapt to a fundamentally changed commercial landscape. And we have continued to struggle to demonstrate that marketing can and does make a difference, to both our customers and our businesses.

Just as Apple did in the late 1990s, we must start to think very differently about our businesses and about our marketing. We must be bold enough to fundamentally shift our thinking from what we do to why it matters, moving our perspective from 'inside-out' – from the marketing tasks that focus on what we manufacture or sell – to 'outside-in' – encompassing how our customers feel about us and what we as a business want to achieve, not over months but over years.

Just like Apple, this means getting back to the fundamentals of marketing – which have not changed – and which I explore in Part Two.

Essential steps to *think different*

We must first *think different* before we can *do different*. But thinking different is not easy; it involves both time and effort, and it can be exhausting. Because thinking different is very uncomfortable for most B2B marketers. It means questioning the accepted norms for marketing within our organizations, and that ultimately means questioning our own expertise, even admitting that there may be many things we don't know. Importantly, it means not simply accepting the obvious and easiest, but working hard to ensure we are exposed to multiple perspectives instead of merely those that validate our existing thinking.

Most of all, in order to *think different* we need to be infinitely curious; we must continually question everything we think we know and what everyone else takes for granted. When we question, we discover new things, open ourselves to new possibilities and increase our knowledge. New knowledge brings new opportunities and new ideas, and paves the way for doing different. This is how we make a difference, how we create impact and become memorable, forging those lasting connections among our customers and across our organizations.

Thinking different is also about understanding why we think the way we do, and making a conscious effort to create an environment that enables new thinking. In B2B marketing we are so busy doing that we don't take enough time, if any, to simply stop and think about or discuss what we're doing and why.

How many of us attend marketing team meetings that focus solely on what we're currently doing or just about to do? We need to make the time and give ourselves the space to think, both on our own and within groups. I don't mean brainstorming sessions, which tend to focus on the same things, just done a bit differently; I mean team sessions where we look honestly at the thinking – the logic, the rationale and the emotion – behind what we do.

Where do we start? Five habits to nurture

The first step is taking a conscious decision to *think different* about B2B marketing. We can start with these five habits:

1. **Schedule thinking time** – for ourselves and together with our teams, on a consistent and regular basis.
2. **Think big** – outside of our marketing silos, about the big issues we're facing as B2B marketers.

3 **Listen well** – we need to take people along with us and give everyone a chance to contribute.
4 **Take responsibility** – don't make excuses; we must find and implement practical, workable solutions to overcome the challenges that are stopping us.
5 **Be accountable** – as individuals and as teams for making specific change happen.

Next steps: Five questions and five actions

Finally, we need to start asking some very tough questions and then take action to answer those questions in meaningful ways (Table 3.1).

Table 3.1 Think different Q&A

Five questions to ask	Five actions to take
How well do I know my customers?	Don't make assumptions about your customers; don't assume that you know who they are or what their needs and issues are. Talk to your sales people and find ways to talk directly to your prospects and customers.
Do I understand how my customers buy?	Map your customers' buyer journey: think beyond specific buyers, consider everyone involved in the purchase decision as well as their influencers, and be sure to include sales in the exercise.
Am I marketing *at* my business or *with* my business?	Marketing should not happen in a vacuum – engage and partner proactively with sales to align objectives and agree all marketing activity and plans.
Do I have marketing myopia (am I focusing on the wrong things)?	Ignore the herd and don't obsess about the latest marketing fads; focus on what's of value to your customers and hold every marketing task and channel to the same measurement standard.
Does this matter?	Clearly articulate both the customer and business outcome you want to achieve and agree this with your leadership.

PART TWO
Do different

FALLACY 2

The marketing plan is the marketing strategy.

Only 37 per cent of marketers in the US and
40 per cent in the UK have a strategy.
CONTENT MARKETING INSTITUTE, 2017

Getting back to B2B marketing basics

04

For years now, too many B2B marketers have been completely focused on tactics and channels, with little or no alignment to our brand, our strategy (if we have one!) or our customers. Mark Ritson calls this the 'tactification of marketing', and if it's any consolation to B2B marketers, it's happening in the B2C world as well.

The constant introduction of new technology is spawning new tactics and channels at a pace with which we can no longer keep up. Every day it seems there is something new and different that we need to get to grips with and incorporate into our marketing activity. And let's face it, we're overwhelmed by it all.

So, what should we do?

The four fundamentals for B2B marketing success

The 2016 High Performance B2B Marketing Benchmarking Report found that 94 per cent of B2B marketers surveyed felt there are four key elements vital to marketing success – brand, strategy, customers and measurement. And yet, the findings of the survey clearly show that while B2B marketers know what's required for success, their focus is elsewhere.

A summary of the findings show that:

- *A startling 57 per cent of high performers and 75 per cent of the rest are working without a clearly defined brand, and even fewer actually have a brand strategy.*

What this means is that without a deep understanding of our brand and strategy, there is simply no way we (or anyone else in the organization) will be able to deliver a coherent, impactful, ongoing story over time about who we are as a business and why it matters.

- *68 per cent of high performers and less than half (46 per cent) of the rest have a marketing strategy and goals that are aligned to the business.*

Two-thirds might sound like a pretty good finding. There has been other research that puts this percentage even lower. But without strategy, marketing remains a series of isolated tactics, and this disconnect between strategy and tactics is deeply troubling.

- *Only 55 per cent of high performers and a shocking 20 per cent of the rest responded that their marketing department has a good understanding of the customer.*

We simply do not know our customers very well in B2B and this finding explains our continuing focus on what we do and what matters to us, instead of what's important to our customers.

- *According to the survey, only 17 per cent of marketers are able to measure marketing's contribution to the wider business.*

This isn't actually surprising as it highlights the ongoing debate about ROI and marketing's continuing efforts to deliver 'value'. I discuss B2B marketing ROI in more detail later on in this chapter.

This report suggests that in B2B marketing we don't understand our brands, we don't have a strategy, our customers are an enigma and we don't know how to measure the value we bring to our organizations. It highlights that we talk the talk but don't actually walk the walk; in other words, we know what's required for marketing success, yet our marketing focus remains elsewhere.

It is often a vicious circle. Many B2B marketers feel bound by what we've always done – even if we know better – because our business doesn't really understand what marketing can and should achieve. Yet the underlying challenge is that instead of doing different things, most often we talk about 'educating' the business about what we already do and trying to convince them that what we're doing is what's of value.

We must realign our thinking about marketing; it's not our business that needs to understand marketing, it's marketing that needs to understand the business.

And we can start by getting back to the marketing fundamentals of brand, strategy, customers and measurement, so we are able to think and do differently from what we've always thought and done.

Who am I? The brand conundrum in B2B

How many B2B marketers can clearly and concisely articulate their organization's brand or purpose?

Sure, we can point to the expression of our visual identity – logo, colour palettes, strapline. But what about the psychological and emotional aspects of our brands – all those perceptions and associations within the hearts and minds of our customers? We know that branding involves so much more than a logo, colour palette and strapline. Yet in B2B, this is where our branding efforts often end.

I used Apple as a case study in Part One of this book and it remains a powerful illustration of understanding and articulating our brands. This campaign was so remarkable because it unambiguously articulated and celebrated the soul of the Apple brand – that creative people with passion, in all walks of life, can change the world, in large ways and small. It redefined what creativity can mean – taking it out of the realm of the 'artsy' – and applied it to science, to business, to everyday human achievements. And it spoke to some very compelling human truths and aspirations.

But we have to remember that this wasn't just emotional grandstanding. Apple was very careful to align this big thinking with what they sell. In essence, Apple's core message transformed from one about cool technology to one about *providing the tools that will go wherever your imagination takes you*. That's pretty powerful, no matter who you are or what you do.

However, understanding and articulating our brands and what they stand for, and aligning our marketing activity to that brand promise, is a huge challenge for B2B.

This brand conundrum is further confused by all the recent focus on organizational purpose.

Understanding purpose – start with Why

Common wisdom has long held that the sole purpose of business is to make money and increase shareholder value. Yet our organizations are part of wider society and they wield enormous power that influences the world we live in. Of course, even the greatest companies must be profitable to survive. But the choices they make in how they do so have an impact far beyond profits and shareholder value.

In 2009, Simon Sinek published what has become a global bestselling book about leadership – *Start with Why: How great leaders inspire everyone*

Figure 4.1 The Golden Circle

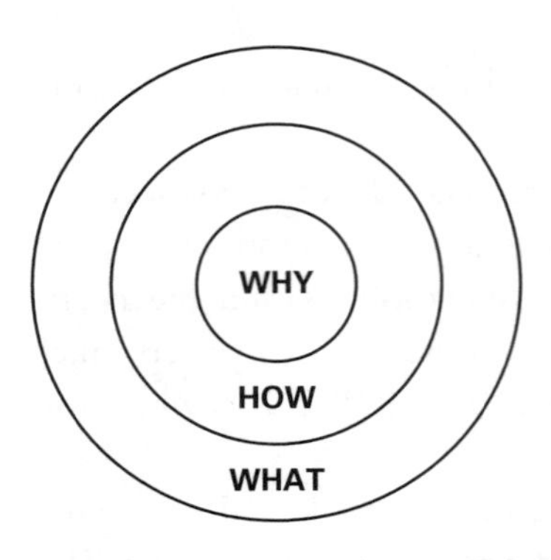

WHAT

Every organization on the planet knows WHAT they do. These are products they sell or the services they offer.

HOW

Some organizations know HOW they do it. These are the things that make them special or set them apart from their competition.

WHY

Very few organizations know WHY they do what they do. WHY is not about making money. That's a result. It's a purpose, cause or belief. It's the very reason your organization exists.

SOURCE Adapted from Sinek (2009)

to take action. On 28 September 2009, he gave what is now a famous TED Talk to a local TEDx Puget Sound audience, which has since had almost 30 million views. In his book and this talk, he introduced his concept of the 'Golden Circle' (Figure 4.1), and perhaps the most challenging point he made is that, 'People don't buy what you do; they buy why you do it.' In other words, we do business with, and buy from, people we like to do business with, whose values align to our own, and to whom we feel connected at an essential, emotional level.

Sinek's premise with his Golden Circle is that, as organizations and people, we think, act and communicate from outside-in – 'Every single person, every single organization on the planet knows what they do, some know how they do it, but very few people or organizations know why they do what they do.' And by why, he isn't talking about making a profit, he's talking about our underlying purpose as people and organizations, and why our customers should care. Sinek wants us to change our perspective; instead of starting with What we do as businesses, he wants us to start with the Why.

This is an important concept for B2B marketers. Because across our industries there is little or no differentiation between our products and services, and the 'why' – if articulated well – can be a powerful motivating factor for our customers.

From a B2B marketing perspective, I think about Sinek's Golden Circle in a slightly different way. I believe that most of our businesses think from the inside-out, starting with what we do (our products and services) and how we do it (as opposed to our competition), and then articulating the why as

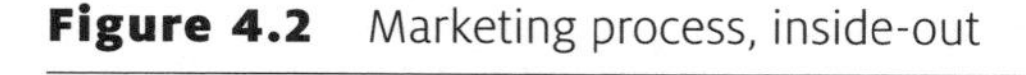

Figure 4.2 Marketing process, inside-out

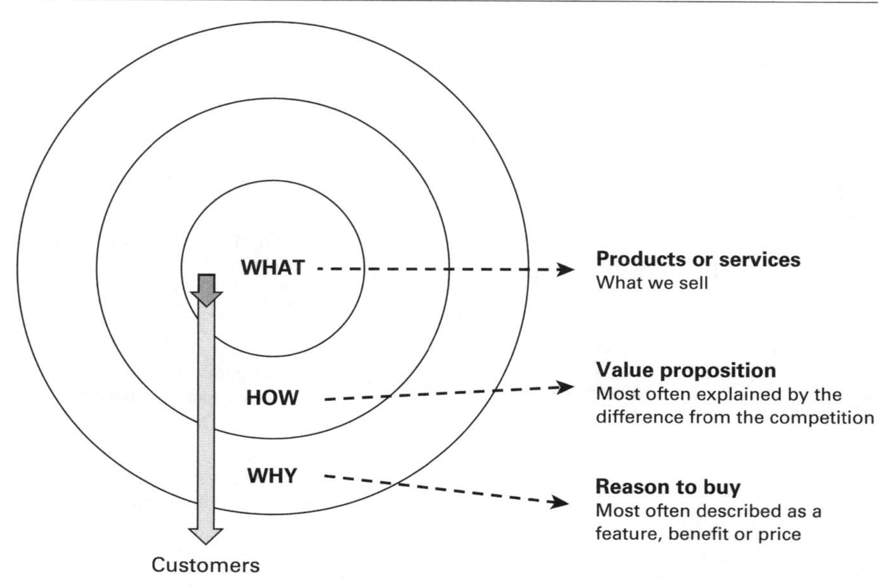

one or more reasons for our customers to buy that product or service, which is almost always in terms of features, benefits and price (Figure 4.2). This perspective is completely focused on what our organizations sell.

But, as I allude to in the Introduction, we need to completely shift our perspective and start first with our customers, asking a fundamental question (Figure 4.3): why does what we do matter to our customers?

This is a major shift in marketing thinking for B2B – from a focus on what we sell (inside-out) to a relentless customer perspective (outside-in) that links our organizational thinking directly to our customers.

Brands with purpose – the Why matters

We spend a lot of our time and energy on the search for purpose and meaning in our lives. Why shouldn't we expect the same from the organizations we do business with – to have a purpose and meaning beyond corporate profits?

What is purpose? Simply put, purpose is the difference between doing a job and understanding why it matters – to ourselves as individuals, to our business stakeholders, to our customers and to the wider world. It's about who we are as a business, what we stand for and what our intrinsic values are beyond what we sell.

Figure 4.3 Marketing process, outside-in

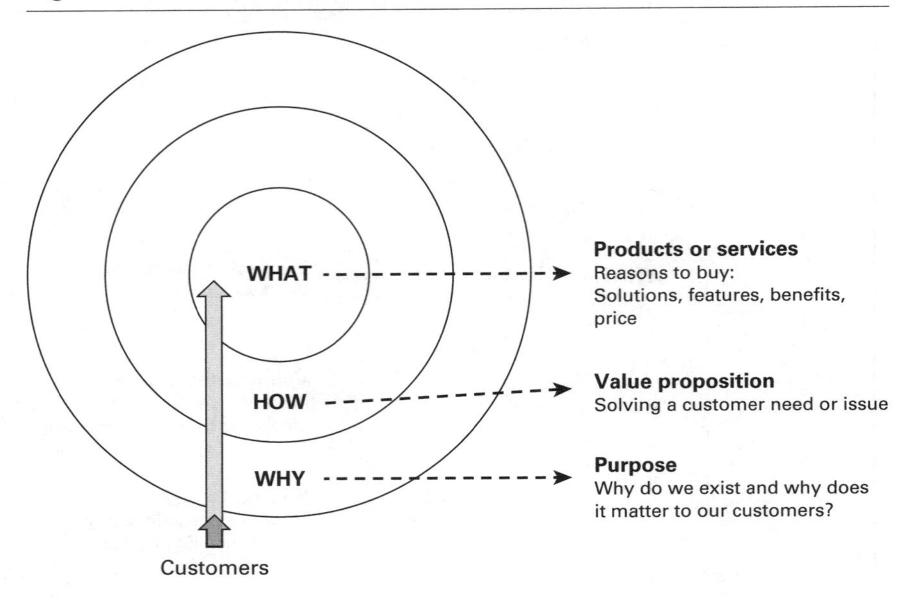

Purpose is not vision, mission or goals (Figure 4.4). The strongest brands are strong because people know what they stand for and how they fit into their lives. They go beyond what they sell and show how they address the real issues impacting individuals and society, providing people with a clear connection between brand promise and brand purpose:

- **Purpose:** the reason your company exists beyond making money – this never changes.
- **Mission:** a master plan for creating value for all of your stakeholders – 5–20 years.
- **Vision:** a shared picture for the success of the mission – 5–20 years.
- **Goal:** a long-term primary outcome resulting from your company mission and vision – 3–5 years.

Marc Benioff, CEO of Salesforce.com, has famously said that the purpose of business isn't just about creating profits for shareholders – it's also about improving the world:

> It's my belief that businesses are the greatest platforms for change and can have an enormous impact on improving the state of the world. [We are] responsible for more than just shareholders. We are accountable for the wellbeing of... our fellow beings on this planet we inhabit. (Benioff, 2016)

Figure 4.4 Purpose, mission, vision and goal

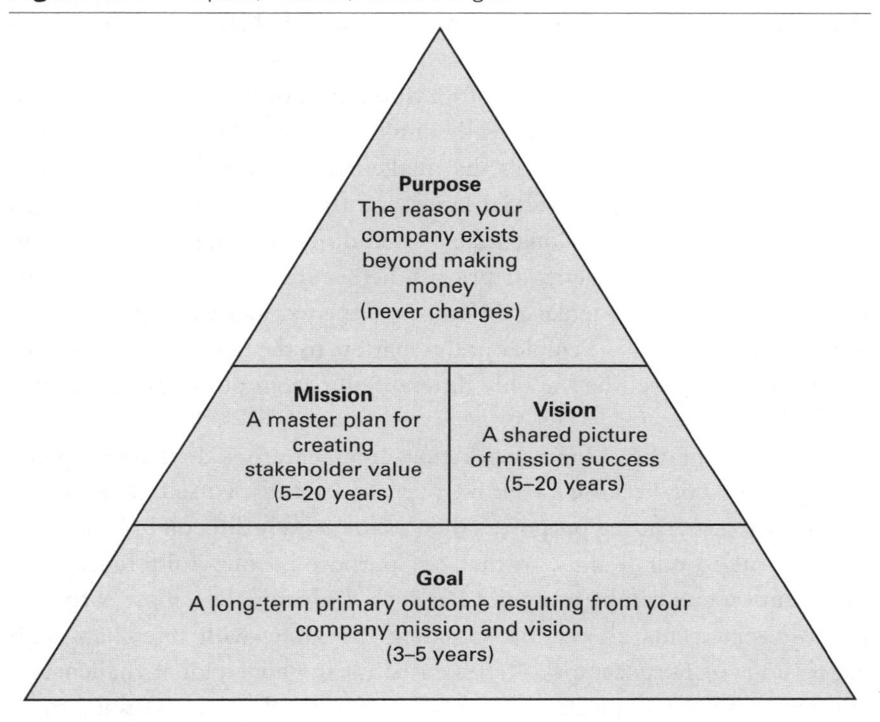

We are increasingly looking for and expecting a wider societal purpose from the organizations we do business with. Havas Media Group produces a Meaningful Brands® index which looks at the benefits brands gain when they are perceived as improving wellbeing and quality of life. Their 2017 research spanned 1,500 brands across 15 industries and 33 countries, and 300,000 people. Their analysis found that those brands with a higher purpose increase their marketing KPIs by up to 137 per cent compared to brands with less meaning. They also increase their share of wallet by nine times and have outperformed the stock market over the past 10 years by 206 per cent. Significantly for 2017, they found that there's a 71 per cent correlation between content effectiveness and brand ranking. That's pretty significant.

Furthermore, PwC's 2016 global CEO Survey found that US CEOs in particular believe that there is a fundamental change happening in how their customers are relating to their businesses. In a summary of their top five findings, PwC found that these CEOs believe 85 per cent of their current customers buy based on cost, convenience and functionality. But, by 2020 their customers will increasingly want to do business with those organizations that go beyond their product or service offering to address wider societal needs – 'customers and other stakeholders will expect business to demonstrate a higher purpose over the coming years'.

There are marketing commentators who have openly ridiculed this focus on purpose, saying that buyers really don't care about higher purpose, they just want products and services that make their lives easier at prices they can afford. But, in a commercial landscape that is becoming increasingly commoditized, we can no longer depend on differentiating our products or services on features, benefits or price. Whether it's in large ways or small, how our organizations make a difference to the world we live in matters. It matters to the people we employ and it matters to the people who buy from us. Purpose may well be the only differentiator from our competitors that we have.

Yet, some of these same marketing commentators do have a point, although it's not because of brand purpose in and of itself. The biggest challenge in articulating purpose is that it's immensely difficult to be authentic and true to our brands, so that our purpose meaningfully reflects our organization and can be recognized as such. Unfortunately, most corporate purpose statements all end up sounding the same, with interchangeable expressions of purpose, too often focused on the huge global challenges – end world hunger, eradicate poverty, cure cancer – that have nothing to do with who we are as organizations. And this is marketing's responsibility – it's not developing brand purpose that is the issue, it's in the marketing execution of communicating that purpose that it has tended to go awry. The unfortunate reality is that articulating purpose has resulted in a large proportion of brands across both the B2B and B2C space being an exercise in banalities, so that there is no differentiation at all.

Furthermore, there is a danger that purpose and corporate social responsibility (CSR) are seen as the same thing, so that purpose becomes the aforementioned banality and CSR remains a departmental function that oversees charitable giving or an annual employee day devoted to participation in a charitable activity. Instead, as with companies like Salesforce.com and Unilever, purpose needs to be understood and practised as fundamental to business strategy and a core component to corporate culture. In the case of Unilever, CEO Paul Polman puts purpose at the centre of everything they do, committing the company to having a positive impact on the environment and public health. Their corporate purpose statement asserts that their success requires 'the highest standards of corporate behaviour towards everyone we work with, the communities we touch, and the environment on which we have an impact' (Unilever, 2017).

Building such a culture is extremely difficult. Rick Wartzman, in an article in *Forbes* in January 2015, describes purpose as having real clarity, not only in the value you bring to customers, but in 'taking responsibility for whatever and whomever you touch'. He explains, for example, that Unilever does this through rigorous measurement of, and reporting on, 'three ambitious goals it aims to reach by 2020: helping more than a billion people across the globe improve their health and wellbeing; halving the environmental footprint of its products; and sourcing 100 per cent of its agricultural raw materials sustainably while enhancing the livelihoods of those working across its supply chain'. And they do this alongside an uncompromising commitment to increasing the size of their business.

When it's done well, purpose enables companies to make a profit as well as make the world we live in a better place, and that's a powerful motivator, for employees as well as customers. According to Dan Pontefract in 'CEOs now believe their customers are expecting a higher sense of purpose' (Forbes, 2016), Craig Dowden, president and founder of Craig Dowden and Associates, a Toronto-based consulting firm, believes purpose is particularly compelling for employees: 'Meaning is becoming increasingly important in today's workplace. Employees are spending more time figuring out their "why". People have lots of choices in terms of where to work. Most of us want to contribute to something beyond ourselves.'

There's a great story about US President John F Kennedy in the early days of NASA: 'What do you do?' the president supposedly asked a janitor during a tour of Cape Canaveral. 'Well, Mr President, I'm helping to put a man on the moon.'

This may or may not have actually happened, though it has become an urban marketing myth, and it's a powerful illustration of this shift in thinking from what we do to why we do it.

And those organizations who get this branding challenge right will take a huge leap ahead of the competition.

The strategy imperative

We create our marketing plans and call them strategy. We start with what we do – the tactics – without doing the hard work upfront about why we're implementing this activity in the first place.

Strategy is the foundation for everything. It articulates the approach we take towards our markets and provides both clarity and purpose around what we do – and perhaps more importantly, what we don't do. A marketing strategy organizes our thinking and thus our actions around what is most important for our business, enabling us to develop and execute marketing plans that actually make a difference.

Yet we constantly use the two terms interchangeably and incorrectly.

The difference between strategy and plans

I want to be very clear here: strategy and planning are fundamentally different and they each have a distinct purpose: strategy is about outcomes (what we want to achieve and how we succeed), while plans are about outputs (what we do):

- A **strategy** is the approach we take to achieve a long-term primary goal – an outcome.
- A **plan** is the detailed set of short-term activities – outputs – that encompass specific objectives and tactics that support the strategy:
  - An *objective* is a measurable step we take to achieve a strategy.
  - A *tactic* is a tool we use in pursuing an objective associated with a strategy.

We also need to understand that business strategy and marketing strategy are very different yet related. It seems obvious, but marketing must be aligned to and support the business strategy. And yet, without even having a marketing strategy, too many conversations I have about strategy with B2B marketers are about how marketing needs to have a place in the boardroom and influence business strategy. I address this issue further in my discussion of leadership in Chapter 9: 'Should marketing have a seat on the board in B2B?'

Granted, many of our businesses don't have a proper strategy. The leader of a very large and successful business once told me that their strategy was to 'sell stuff'. Let's face it, that's not a strategy. But who are we to discuss business strategy if we don't even fully understand what strategy is and is not?

Then there are those who tell me that their business doesn't have a strategy and ask how they can possibly develop marketing strategy without one. Frankly, this is just another excuse. It is our responsibility as marketing leaders to develop marketing strategy; this is a critical part of our jobs. Even if our business does not have a proper strategy, that does not preclude us from developing our strategy for marketing. However, we can't do this in a vacuum and we must come out of our marketing silos to have meaningful discussions with the business – to understand their objectives and aspirations, their markets and customers, their priorities and both their short-term and long-term needs. This doesn't have to be a discussion about strategy, we just need to ask the right questions and then sit back and listen to the business.

This is so important it bears repetition: A marketing plan is not marketing strategy. Without strategy, plans are just a random set of tactics that may or may not actually achieve anything for the wider business. At best, plans without strategy may realize some short-term targets. At worst, they consume valuable time, budget and energy in the wrong direction, in pursuit of misaligned objectives.

Developing strategy is, in essence, about clearly articulating:

- What is our long-term goal?
- Why do we exist?
- Where will we compete?
- How will we win?

Marketing strategy must always precede planning and must support the business strategy. It is the one effort that will make the most difference in both how our businesses perceive the marketing function and the impact we make in our markets. Because if we don't know where we're going, how will we know if and when we get there?

Six questions that separate strategy and plans

Bear with me for a moment. When I was very young, I loved Rudyard Kipling's *Just So Stories*. One of my favourites was 'The Elephant's Child', which is about curiosity as essential for acquiring new knowledge, having new ideas and developing new abilities. There's a poem in the story that in part goes:

> I keep six honest serving-men
>
> (They taught me all I knew);
>
> Their names are What and Why and When
>
> And How and Where and Who.

What, Why, When, How, Where and Who. These are the basic questions we ask as we explore the world, gather information, invent stories and learn new things, whether as children or adults.

These are also the essential questions that separate our marketing strategy and plans. Simply put, but definitely not simple, strategy is the Where, the How and the Why – where do we want to go, how are we going to get there and why does it matter? The plan is then the What, the When and the Who – what are we going to do, when are we going to do it and who will we engage with?

Strategy is for the long term, no matter how the business environment may change, and should form the touchstone against which every marketing decision is made. The plan is for the short term, agile and flexible, responsive to changing market conditions, but always in complete alignment to the strategy.

This is a critical distinction, because without a destination, how can we even begin to think about what needs to be done to get where we want and need to go?

Why is strategy so hard for B2B marketers?

There is one and only one marketing strategy – not multiple tactical strategies – for each of the organizations we work for. If done well, this strategy will be for the long term – no matter how the commercial landscape may change – and will be one that all marketers in the organization can relate to, forming both the touchstone and the criterion for every marketing activity.

But strategy is hard; and because we don't actually understand strategy – what it is or how to develop it – we default to what we do know, the tactics. We then talk about all these tactics as strategies, plural. We have our digital strategies, our social media strategies, our content strategies, ad infinitum, which are each and every one simply a plan of activity for each tactic or channel. We continue to use our events calendar, our editorial calendars or our website plans as evidence of our marketing team's 'strategies'.

These activities are not strategy. We remain stuck in the tactical execution yet we believe we are being strategic. We simply don't know any better.

There are three very big obstacles that contribute to this ongoing confusion:

1 **What is the role of our marketing leadership?** I have been in meetings with marketing directors of both large and small B2B services organizations. Of course, I always ask about their organization's business strategy and marketing strategy. Too many of these senior marketing people tell

me things such as their marketing strategy is to 'create and disseminate relevant content'. These same marketers invariably cannot articulate their organization's business strategy at all.

Frankly, I'm speechless when this happens. Yet these are not unique occurrences. I'm concerned that our senior people focus on managing the function – the marketing outputs – rather than providing the strategic thinking necessary for the marketing outcomes that are meaningful for the business. I explore this leadership dilemma further in Chapter 9.

2 **Are we training our people how to think?** I mentor a few younger marketing professionals across diverse industries. One of them has been looking for a new job, so I've been coaching them on their CV preparation and interviewing. This person has used the word 'strategy' throughout their CV, yet when I've pressed them for examples of their strategic work, they've given me numerous examples of tactics but could not articulate what strategy meant in the context of their current role, or what it would look like in the role they wanted.

I don't necessarily expect junior marketers to be 'strategic', but I do expect them to begin thinking about what they do – the tactical execution – in the context of the wider marketing strategy. Yet how can they do that if we don't even understand the difference ourselves? In Chapter 8 I look at how we hire and the kind of training we must provide our people at all levels. This also links to the leadership challenge I mentioned above and which I explore further in Chapter 9.

3 **Who are we listening to?** I was recently asked to contribute to an article for a marketing publication that's one of my marketing 'bibles'. They were asking a variety of senior marketing people across industries for their 'top 3 strategies that work every time'. Note the use of language – multiple strategies. When I delved deeper into what the article was meant to explore, it was pretty clear that the article was intended to discover the most effective tactics used by the best marketers. And yet the article was clearly equating tactics and strategy.

I'm uneasy because I constantly see a whole host of articles, blog posts and so-called thought leadership on the subject of marketing strategy which are actually not about strategy at all. The explosion of social networks means that virtually anyone can proclaim themselves a 'marketing expert'. But I rarely see anyone questioning this so-called expertise or challenging the ideas they broadcast.

What's your marketing strategy?

It is imperative that we stop all these random acts of marketing and start the hard work that developing strategy requires. Yet the biggest challenges we face are that too many of us simply do not know where to begin or we overcomplicate the process. We thus default straight to the tactics and skip the critical thinking that's necessary to really make a difference to our businesses.

I'm a great believer in keeping things simple. But simple doesn't mean easy. In Chapter 5, I introduce my 3D Marketing System for Strategy and Planning, deeply exploring my framework that will help you develop and deliver your marketing strategy and plans.

But, as a first step, the next time you have a team meeting, try the following simple exercise.

Team meeting exercise

On separate Post-it notes, take a few minutes and have your people answer these three questions:

1 What is your marketing purpose?
2 What is your marketing goal?
3 How are you going to achieve that goal?

Don't think too much about it, there's no right or wrong answer here, just write down what first comes to mind, or simply put a question mark. Then stick the Post-it notes onto a wall or other surface, and group the responses. What are these responses telling you? Some things to consider:

- **Purpose**: Like Simon Sinek, I always start with Why. In a world where there is very little that distinguishes us from our competitors, purpose can be the real differentiator for organizations. *As a marketing function, we must continually ask ourselves why we are doing what we do and why it matters – to both our organizations and our customers.*
- **Goal**: A goal isn't just about growth; it's a long-term primary outcome that provides a clear direction for our business. *From a marketing perspective, this means thinking about the impact we actually have and the impact we want to have within our business as well as the marketplace.*

- **Strategy**: Strategy is the approach we take that encompasses our purpose in order to achieve our goal. It's NOT the marketing plan; it's NOT the tactics. *It's the fundamental story we tell in the marketplace, articulating our value proposition in a way that differentiates what we do.*

Strategy isn't just words on a page; strategy is the touchstone that every marketer in the organization needs to understand, and against which every single marketing activity must be aligned and measured. And it takes more than tactical marketing expertise – it takes a deep understanding of our customers, our markets and our business.

Customer engagement: winning hearts and minds

In Chapter 2, I spoke about how B2B marketing has been jumping on the customer experience bandwagon and how I see marketing's role in delivering a seamless, integrated experience across channels throughout the buyer journey.

But before we even start to think about 'owning' the end-to-end customer experience across the organization, we have to get the engagement piece right. And if we want to engage our customers in any meaningful way, we have to know them first.

I may be stating the obvious yet again, but it's the obvious that most often gets overlooked. At the beginning of this chapter I pulled out the key findings from the '2016 High Performance B2B Marketing' benchmarking report, which illustrated that we don't know our customers very well at all in B2B. As a reminder, 45 per cent of high performers and fully 80 per cent of the rest of the survey respondents did not think their marketing departments understood their customers.

This is a stark message for us in B2B marketing and goes a long way towards explaining why so much of our marketing activity is not making any kind of impact with our customers.

In past years, we've tried to take a page from the consumer world and make the customer king; we've heard and spoken a lot about customer first, customer focus and customer centricity. These are important concepts for our organizations as we continue to adjust to the social era and change our perspective from inside-out to outside-in. So why don't we know our customers better?

What's the difference between customer experience and customer engagement?

Like so many other words in marketing, 'engagement' has become overused and misinterpreted. Lately it's used most often to define a metric, one that's exclusively digital, and intended to discover if we are holding our customers' attention on our websites. Bounce rate, time on site, social shares, click-throughs, comments and sign-ups are just some of the metrics that supposedly measure 'engagement'.

But customer engagement is really quite different from this narrow view; thinking holistically from a marketing perspective, it's about how we build and maintain relationships with our customers, no matter where they are or what channels and platforms they use. It's about deeply connecting with our customers as people, as individuals, not in a single instance, but over time. And make no mistake, relationships are critical in B2B.

In Chapter 2, I introduced the concept of customer experience, with a definition provided by the *Harvard Business Review*: 'The sum totality of how customers engage with your company and brand, not just as a snapshot in time, but throughout the entire arc of being a customer.' But I found this definition difficult to get my head around because customer experience and customer engagement are not the same.

In 2010, Harley Manning, a Forrester analyst, defined customer experience as, 'How customers perceive their interactions with your company.' This perspective, among others, prompted Paul Greenburg, author and president of a customer strategy consulting company in the United States, to explain the difference between customer experience and customer engagement in an article on the ZDnet website (2015):

- Customer *experience* is 'how a customer feels about a company over time'.
- Customer *engagement* is 'the ongoing interactions between company and customer offered by the company, chosen by the customer'.

Finally, a clear definition that helps us to understand the difference and makes sense of how we think about our customers; not just in the sense of what we do to engage them, but in how they engage with us. Customer experience – the sum totality – is the intangible *perception* that our customers have of our companies, and customer engagement is the tangible *interaction* between customer and company.

Another way of thinking about this is that customer experience is the accumulation of these ongoing interactions (the customer engagement). This accumulation is a total outcome that is measured by customer satisfaction scores, while the engagement itself has different metrics.

This should resonate with B2B marketers. These interactions are what all the marketing tactics are supposed to enable, if integrated and aligned with marketing strategy.

Yet I continue to hear from a lot of B2B marketers that their business doesn't value what they do. My response typically is: if the business doesn't value what you do, then try doing something different that they *will* value. It has, however, brought home to me how disconnected marketing is from the business, and how much of what we do really adds value. Because we've become so intent on what we do, there is an overriding attitude – from both marketers and the business – that marketing is something that's done *to* the business, not *with* the business.

As marketers, we typically create content as a foundation for the marketing programmes and campaigns that we use to engage our customers. But what if we did the engagement piece first and then created the content?

Let me give you an example from my own experience as an in-house marketer in B2B. I was working with a new leader for a new part of a business where marketing had no previous traction or credibility. At first, all the business wanted was a website that would tell our customers about us and our products and services. Sound familiar? But instead of hurrying ahead with the task – the website – I spent a lot of time asking questions and listening to the business about what they really wanted to achieve, where the opportunity was for them in the market and, most importantly, who they wanted to engage with.

What came out of these discussions was a multi-channel programme over a two-year period that began not with a website or a publication – not with content creation – but with direct engagement with customers, where we listened to and explored the issues that mattered to them. And it was a real eye-opener for the business. For the first time, this part of the business was able to elevate the conversation beyond what we 'sold', and by doing so made a real difference to how our customers perceived us. In fact, one influential buyer had not been favourably disposed towards us, and had been pretty blunt, telling us (and others in the market) that they bought from a competitor because we 'didn't understand their issues'. As an immediate result of our engagement activity, he asked us if we would be interested in having further discussions with him. Well, yes!

Of course, it was then up to me and my team to create wider impact and further engagement with the rest of the programme. And I did eventually develop that website. But by doing something very different from what had been done before with the business – by starting with customer engagement – I was able to create immediate opportunities for the business as well as eventually create content that was much more relevant and engaging for our customers.

The end of ROI as we know it?

> There is nothing quite so useless, as doing with great efficiency, that which should not be done at all. (Peter Drucker, 1963)

Measuring what we do is critical to understanding if we're actually doing the right things, instead (as the great Peter Drucker wrote) of just doing things right and – with 'great efficiency' – still doing those things which are no longer relevant or important to our customers or our business.

Of course, we'd all love to quantify our marketing activity with a single number – this amount of marketing spend generated that amount of revenue. But return on investment (ROI) in the B2B world is not as straightforward as that. The sales cycle in B2B is often a lengthy one, and there are many complex interactions that happen at all levels throughout the organization before the sale is finally closed. ROI in this sense doesn't give us insight into these dimensions, nor does it tell us what's working, what's not, or why. It doesn't tell us what kind of impact we're making in our markets or whether we're achieving the level of customer engagement we're aiming for.

Resetting the 'value' agenda in B2B marketing

What are we really trying to measure with our ROI?

It may be unconventional, but I don't think we should be measuring marketing ROI at all any more. At least, not as we currently do; we need to be measuring it differently, and even with all this technology at our fingertips, we still don't have the right tools.

I'm not saying that we shouldn't be measuring our marketing activity. I'm simply saying that we are measuring the wrong things. ROI as we've long known it has disintegrated into a numbers tally and a tick-box exercise, rather than a real value calculation. We've become so obsessed with all this 'Big Data' that we've lost sight of what we're trying to measure.

Because we all know that numbers can be made to mean just about anything. Just because we *can* measure something doesn't mean we should be measuring it, or that it has meaning for our business. I've worked in companies where every marketing campaign is a resounding success, and we have the numbers to prove it! But marketing 'success' is all relative, dependent upon what we're really trying to achieve. Data is not insight, numbers are meaningless without context, and we are not yet doing the real work of what all this actually signifies.

By not looking beyond the numbers, we are undermining what marketing is really intended to achieve and thus also weakening the perceived value of marketing to the organization. What value is good ROI if the broader marketing and organizational goals aren't being met?

So, what should we be measuring? This is not an easy question to answer. But the first step is to stop thinking in terms of marketing outputs and start thinking in terms of marketing outcomes; in other words, start thinking about what we're actually achieving in terms of overall business contribution. This means profoundly resetting the 'value' agenda with our stakeholders. By being very clear about what the purpose and expected outcomes are, and agreeing fundamentally different measures of success, we may be better able to understand the real impact that marketing is having over time on our bottom line.

I think of ROI as Relationships, One Business and Impact – in other words, are we building the relationships we want with our customers, are we going to market as a single organization instead of multiple product or service lines, and are we making an impact, with our customers and on the wider market?

What this means, at least for now, is that we must change the conversation and start to have profoundly different kinds of discussions with our business about what marketing success looks like. Otherwise we run the risk of achieving some great numbers for our marketing activity, but not the core objectives, which are about engaging in meaningful and relevant ways that win hearts and minds, and ultimately win work.

Zero-based budgeting – a new approach to marketing planning

> If you want something new, you have to stop doing something old.
> (Peter Drucker, nd)

A bigger budget won't make you a better marketer, but zero-based budgeting (ZBB) just might.

Lack of marketing budget is consistently cited as a significant barrier to success by many B2B marketers. Yet I always argue that big budgets may be as much of a challenge as small ones. Because more doesn't always equate to better; it's not the size of our budgets that matters, it's what we do with them.

When Unilever announced in January 2016 that it was implementing a zero-based budgeting (ZBB) approach across their entire organization – including marketing – marketers and the marketing media were in a bit of an uproar. It's unfortunate that ZBB has traditionally been used as a cost-cutting measure, because it's actually a powerful tool that can help marketers realign their strategy and challenge ingrained, ineffective approaches to the marketing planning and budgeting process. And most importantly, integrate accountability, and thus meaningful measures, into our marketing spend.

Because ZBB is a strategic approach towards planning and budgeting that begins from square one – the zero – every time. What this means is that we need to forget about what we did last year and focus on what we need to achieve for the business this year. It starts with the strategy, not the plan. It starts with marketing talking to the business to get to grips with what they want and need to achieve, then develop a marketing plan that is accountable to the business. Only then do we look at what budget is necessary to support that.

This is a very different approach for most of us, who are used to having our budgets allocated based on our budget the previous year, regardless of whether that marketing activity was successful or effective.

ZBB forces us to plan and budget more effectively – and that's not the same as cutting costs – so that we take a good hard look at what we do and why we're doing it. ZBB can be an empowering process for marketing and has so many advantages and benefits, including:

- **Changing perceptions** about marketing within the business: by having clear communication, collaboration and agreement upfront with all stakeholders on the marketing strategy, goals and objectives – and what measures will be used to identify success – marketing then becomes an activity that's done in partnership *with* the business, not in isolation *from* the business.

- **Accountability:** by embracing ZBB we become accountable for our marketing investment choices and that accountability gives us what we need to demonstrate value within the business.
- **New ways of thinking:** ZBB challenges us to become better marketers, who think as well as do, pushing the boundaries of what marketing can and should be, and educating ourselves on where we need to go next. Traditional marketing planning and budgeting too often is draining and frustrating, and allow too many of us to get away with mediocrity.
- **Focus:** so that we stop doing those activities 'we've always done' that are no longer making an impact; we have simply got to stop doing so much 'stuff' and start doing fewer, more meaningful, impactful activities – but do them better, deeper, wider and for far longer.

Even if our companies aren't doing it, marketing can and should be embracing a ZBB approach. Because simply having a bigger budget won't drive us to the kind of strategic thinking that will make us better marketers.

An introduction to 3D marketing 05

In the previous chapter, I explored the difference between marketing strategy and plans, and why it's critical that we not only understand the difference, but are able to develop our strategy and subsequent plans so that we deliver maximum value for both our business and customers.

Marketing is not done in a vacuum. The most successful marketers give themselves the time and space to carefully review their ongoing marketing activity as well as revisit the assumptions that underpin their marketing strategy and plans. And they do this *with* their business as well as their teams, so that they gain a deeper understanding of customer needs and challenges, and business objectives, as well as what's working and what's not.

Marketing strategy and planning are irrevocably intertwined. The most brilliant strategy is worthless without the ability to execute. And without strategy, plans are – at best – a random set of tactics that may or may not have an impact on the business or – at worst – a whole lot of useless noise.

Yet as we discovered in Chapter 4, strategy is hard, and planning is more than a calendar of individual tactics executed over time.

A 3D Marketing System for Strategy and Planning

I'm a great believer in process, without being wedded to the process. Process gives us an environment and structure for our thinking, without which we're less able to reach the outcome we want. Have you ever attended a meeting that didn't have an agenda? And, at the end, wondered what the purpose of the meeting actually was or what was accomplished? Process enables a direction of travel and signposts for our thinking; they are the steps we take to get where we want to go. By not being wedded to the process we create a safe environment in which to experiment and step outside of our comfort zones.

Over my 25 years in B2B marketing I've created a system that's an effective process for structuring our thinking – I call it my *3D Marketing System for Strategy and Planning*. It's a simple framework that eliminates the overwhelming nature of developing strategy and subsequent plans, and breaks the process down into easily manageable components. It does take hard work.

Developing our marketing strategy and plans – differentiate, develop, deliver

Marketing is ultimately responsible for achieving three main outcomes:

1. differentiating our business from the competition in the hearts and minds of our customers;
2. developing a marketing strategy that is aligned to and supports the business strategy; and
3. delivering that strategy through an integrated set of plans that align tactics and channels to achieve marketing and organizational goals.

Again, this seems fairly obvious, but as I've mentioned before, we often tend to overlook what may be most obvious. And it's important to continually revisit these underlying assumptions so that we can keep our focus on what matters.

Figure 5.1 3D Marketing System for B2B Strategy and Planning

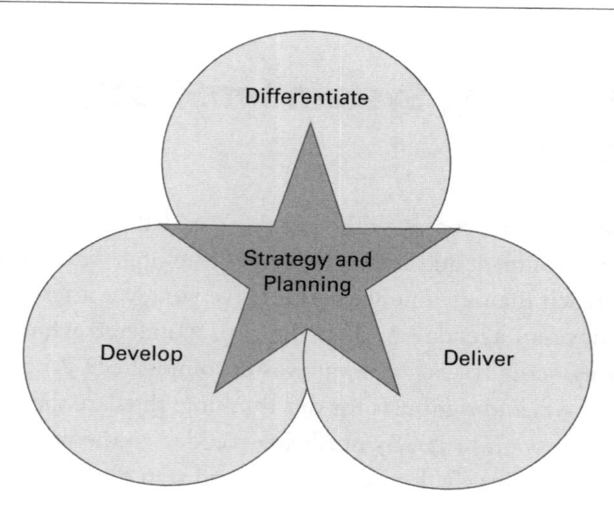

Strategy first – a four-step framework

It all begins with strategy. My 3D Marketing System encompasses four steps for developing strategy – focusing on our Goals, our Why, our Where and our How.

Step One – articulating our goal

Strategy is the approach we take to achieve our goals. Remember, a goal is a long-term primary outcome that provides the direction for what we do as marketers. So, our initial step before even starting to develop marketing strategy is to articulate our goals. We may have a single long-term goal or we may have multiple goals. But either way, it involves answering three key questions for marketing:

1 What is/are the marketing outcome(s) we want to achieve?
2 What do we as marketers and our marketing function want to be famous for, as a whole?
3 Over what period of time?

Clearly defined and articulated marketing goals should be aligned to the business goals, ensuring our marketing teams understand and unify around what matters most to our organizations.

Figure 5.2 3D marketing strategy

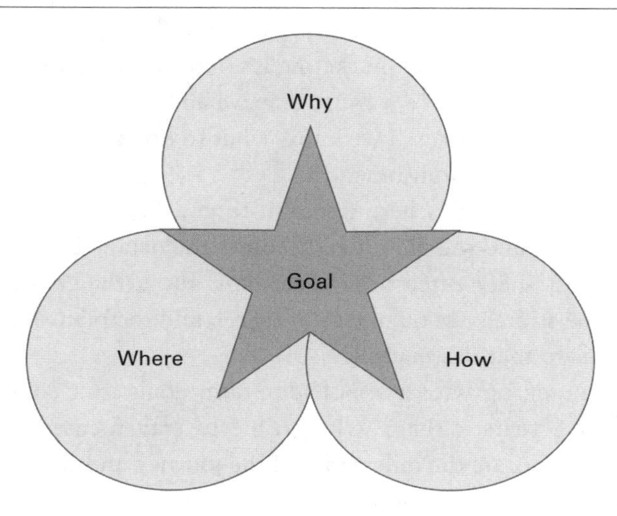

Goals are not objectives. Typically, most B2B marketers formulate their goals within one or more of the following areas:

- building brand awareness;
- generating leads;
- establishing thought leadership;
- launching new products or services;
- targeting new customers;
- increasing customer engagement;
- improving internal communications;
- contributing to revenue.

These are objectives, not goals, and – as with strategy and plans – we must stop confusing the two. (I discuss objectives further in the context of our individual and team objectives in Chapter 7.)

Determining marketing goals within the context of strategy development involves a lot of introspection, and devoting proper time to it can be difficult in our B2B output-based marketing environment. But articulating goals is about envisioning what we want the future of marketing to be in our organizations. Having a clear goal or goals enables us to see a future-state; it helps our people to think beyond their day-to-day tasks and understand how what they do day-to-day contributes to that future. This then leads to better overall performance and productivity, with less waste of time and energy on those activities that don't support the achievement of those goals. And that improves not only overall marketing success, but also the perception within the business of how and what marketing is contributing to the business.

If we don't know what we want to achieve and who we want to be, and set a timeframe for it, how will we know what to do in order to get there or how to measure its accomplishment?

Simply put, the goal is where we want to go, the strategy is how we're going to get there, and the plan then becomes the detailed steps we need to take. An analogy that's often used is to think about the goal as a holiday destination, the strategy as the mode of travel, and the plan as the itinerary that will get us to that destination.

But just coming up with a set of long-term goals isn't enough. A year, three years, five years... that's a long time to stay focused. Goal-setting should also incorporate the milestones of the journey and the measures that will be used at each step of the way.

Once we understand our long-term goals and the timeframe for achieving them, we can begin to get to grips with articulating the core elements of our strategy.

Step Two – articulating our why

The Why is our purpose. I discussed purpose in depth in Chapter 4 in the context of corporate purpose. But it is just as important to understand our purpose as marketers and as a marketing function. Articulating our Why involves answering three key questions:

1. Why do we exist?
2. What do we stand for and Who do we want to be?
3. Why does this matter (what is our impact on our customers and our business)?

Our Why then forms the foundation for everything we may do as marketers.

I discuss the central purpose of the B2B marketing function in depth in Chapter 7, because purpose is an extremely difficult concept for everyone to get to grips with. But for the moment, consider the parable of the three stonecutters (author unknown):

The three stonecutters

A traveller came across three stonecutters working in a quarry and asked them what they were doing. The first stopped what he was doing and replied, 'I'm making a living.' The second kept on hammering while he said, 'I'm doing the best job of stonecutting in the entire county.' The third looked up with a glow in his eyes and said, 'I'm building a cathedral.'

The first stonecutter is involved in a simple value exchange, earning a pay cheque by completing a task. The measure of success is the amount of output. The second stonecutter is also focused on the task, but with the added dimensions of quality and competition, as measured against the stonecutter's peers. But the third stonecutter sees and understands the work as part of a larger whole, of what will be achieved over time by all these stones, one on top of the other.

It is this perspective, this understanding of what we are building, that defines our Why, which is our purpose for marketing.

Step Three – articulating our where

The Where has to do with where we are competing. We simply must understand our markets, our customers, and our positioning within those markets so that we have a clear understanding of where we are now and where we want to go. We then segment and prioritize those markets we will actively pursue and engage with.

A great exercise at this point is the traditional mapping of the competitor landscape and positioning within that landscape, so that we can clearly see where our business is now and where we may want to go. Again, we must answer three key questions:

1. What market(s) are we in and what is our positioning within each?
2. Where do we grow (have we segmented the market)?
3. Where will we focus our marketing investment (which segment or segments will we select or prioritize)?

These questions and the competitor landscaping exercise ensure we completely understand our organization's priorities and are in alignment with the business.

Another useful exercise is that of customer journey mapping. And it's critical that we do this mapping with our salespeople. As a marketing function, we simply cannot be everywhere our customers are. Yet too many of us try to do too much, which only results in spreading our activity so thin that we have no chance of making a consistent and sustainable impact with our customers over time.

Mapping the customer's buying journey creates a visual representation of a customer's or segment's buying behaviours and decision-making processes. It will never be an exact representation of individual behaviours, but it will provide better clarity on where and how long our customers might spend in specific phases, enabling us to concentrate our efforts where we might be able to have the most impact.

Articulating our Where is fundamentally about making choices and prioritizing our marketing efforts. It's an important step in understanding where marketing will focus and will help us to better determine what we will and won't do.

Step Four – articulating our how

There is little, if any, differentiation between many of our products and services in today's market. Our customers have a lot of choice and they can just as easily buy from our competitors, for the same features, price, quality and service. So why should they buy our products and services?

The How is the approach we take towards our markets and involves clearly articulating our value proposition and the overriding story we want to tell in the marketplace. This latter is really important because there may be many stories we could potentially tell. The three questions we must ask are:

1 How will we go to market? In other words, what is our value proposition?
2 What resources, capabilities and support systems do we need?
3 How do we align and integrate across our business?

Keep in mind that we aren't talking tactics or channels here; those are the details that go into our plans, which I discuss later in this chapter. Our How is fundamentally about our brand, clearly articulating our value proposition for our customers as well as for marketing within our organization. It involves deciding on and developing the story or stories we want to tell, coherently and consistently across our organizations, so that we go to market with a single, harmonious and differentiated voice.

As far back as 2013, our B2B buyers were already telling us that the majority of B2B organizations were interchangeable to them. According to research at the time, '86 per cent of B2B buyers saw no real difference between suppliers' (CEB and Google, 2013).

We haven't seen much change over the years; we all adopt the same language, the same overused buzzwords. If we took our company logos off all our marketing materials, would our customers be able to tell the difference? We simply don't spend enough time crafting our messages and honing our propositions into something that is meaningful for our customers and sounds different from our competitors.

Furthermore, we need to realistically assess the resources that are required, from a human, financial and systems perspective. Beyond the marketing budget, where are the capability and capacity gaps? What marketing structure and infrastructure do we need to deliver on our marketing commitments? Sometimes we need to make some very tough decisions.

I once headed up the marketing for a newly created cross-company marketing function focused on a specific industry sector within a much larger organization. This new marketing function brought together the marketing teams associated with the separate product groups that were independently targeting the same sector, with very different messages and propositions, and without a concerted strategy. Alongside the business, I developed an integrated marketing strategy that changed the marketing direction, adopting a thematic approach to the industry's issues and challenges, matching the marketing priorities with the business priorities. This meant that we had to stop doing a lot of things that had always been done and start doing some very different things. And the team I inherited did not have the right skills or experience in order to make the necessary shift.

I discuss the skills, habits and qualities that make a great B2B marketer in Chapter 7. But if we are going to become the kinds of marketing leaders our B2B organizations want and expect, we have to do some hard thinking about the teams we need to make that happen. Because without those teams, we will never be able to deliver on our marketing promises.

Putting it all together – the strategic narrative

Even though we are attempting to articulate our marketing strategy, it's critical to ensure that our strategy aligns to and supports the delivery of the business strategy. We must be able to put our business strategy alongside our marketing strategy and clearly see this alignment, with narratives that complement one another. I've found that this is best expressed by completing these sentences and putting them side-by-side (Table 5.1).

For example, I once worked with a B2B organization during an economic downturn. This business made a strategic decision to stay in a part of the market that suddenly stopped buying and from which the competition was exiting. The business made this decision because they believed the market would come back more strongly than before and wanted to ensure they maintained relationships within that market and were well positioned when the market was prepared to buy again.

The narrative – which I've anonymized – for the business strategy and subsequent marketing strategy went something like the one shown in Table 5.2.

Table 5.1 The strategic narrative

B2B brand	B2B marketing
Why = Purpose = Soul of the brand We are a business dedicated to...	**Why = Purpose = Soul of marketing** Our marketing is dedicated to...
Where = Markets, positioning and segmentation For organizations/people with x need who...	**Where = Markets, positioning and segmentation** For x part of our business and/or x customers who...
How = Approach to market and value proposition We do this by...	**How = Approach to market and value proposition** We do this by...

Table 5.2 Example of the strategic narrative

B2B business	B2B marketing
We are a business dedicated to helping solve some of the most pressing challenges being faced by our most iconic institutions during difficult times. We do this by bringing decades of experience and expertise across industries and, together with others, develop new thinking and ideas that will provide practical, workable solutions to the industry's most urgent needs.	We are dedicated to facilitating the debate around the big issues being faced in this industry. Working with stakeholders across the industry and other third parties, we deliver a programme of research and deliberation that supports our business and leads to new thinking within the market.

By articulating such a narrative, and agreeing it with the business, the marketing team became very clear about what needed to be achieved. This then provided the structure for the marketing plans, so that they could make decisions about what they would – and importantly, what they would not – do for and with the business.

The marketing plan and its go-to-market ecosystem

The marketing plan is the activity that delivers the marketing strategy. In B2B, we tend be very good at delivering this activity, but I suspect that most of us could be much, much better at developing our marketing plans.

As we come under mounting pressure to 'prove' marketing value within our B2B organizations, the marketing planning process has become increasingly and overly complicated. Furthermore, it's too often regarded as a chore, imposed upon us from above. We go through the motions because it's required of us in order to secure our annual budgets. In fact, time and again I see marketers start the planning process with the budget – this is how much I'm going to ask for, based on what I had last year – and then backfilling with the tactics that use up this budget.

> The marketing plan isn't and shouldn't be based on budget!

Another challenge is the complex and changing nature of the B2B commercial landscape. Many of the marketers I speak with tell me they feel that their marketing planning efforts are wasted, that the market is moving so fast that any plan quickly becomes redundant. They use terms like 'flexible' and 'agile' when describing what they do, when – without a plan – they actually just end up being reactive to the demands of the business.

> If you fail to plan, you are planning to fail! (attributed to Benjamin Franklin)

How many of us actually look at our annual marketing plans throughout the year? Once we submit our plans and secure our budget, how many of us tick the 'done' box and put it in a drawer, never to be looked at again, except perhaps as the template for the following year?

In the daily hustle and bustle of our marketing lives, it's hard to turn our attention to the bigger picture. Most of us are so caught up in the urgency of delivery mode that we simply don't take the time to do the kind of thinking that is a core discipline of our jobs. Marketing planning then becomes a by-product to the 'real work' of marketing. We become better at the 'doing' and our planning skills atrophy.

But, deciding what to do and how to do it is our greatest challenge as marketers. And even though we know that all plans are imperfect – how can we know what's going to happen over the course of the year? – if we don't plan, if we don't have a clear idea of where we want to go and how to get there, how can we know if we're doing the right things in the right ways?

The marketing plan is an essential tool of our trade, so much more than just a useful discipline or a necessary chore, especially when marketing is going through such profound change. The planning process gives us time for the high-level thinking that provides the real value to the business, pulling us out of the day-to-day urgent and important activity into the critical thinking that will make a difference to what marketing can and should achieve throughout the year.

By its very nature, a marketing plan is fluid, continually revised and refined over the course of the year. Its core function is to remind ourselves of where we've been and where we're going, ensuring alignment to the business plan and forming the foundation for the detailed project plans that come after the initial planning process.

Most importantly, developing the marketing plan is an opportunity to engage deeply with the business, so that it's done *with* the business, not *to* the business. By constantly going back to our plans during the course of a year, carefully adjusting and honing in response to market or business dynamics, it gives us further opportunities to have ongoing conversations with the business. It's these conversations that often act as a catalyst for the really big ideas that have the potential to make marketing memorable in the hearts and minds of our customers.

Isn't this worthy of our time and effort? But we have got to keep it simple if we're going to be taken seriously by our businesses. I see way too many marketing plans that are dozens and dozens of pages long, filled with excruciating detail that is more fluff than content, as if the sheer number of pages will testify to the strength of the plan. Our stakeholders just don't have the time or interest to wade through pages and pages of marketing justification.

It's useful to envision the marketing plan in terms of the entire go-to-market ecosystem, and my 3D Marketing System encompasses three core elements for developing the marketing plan (Figure 5.3).

The go-to-market ecosystem describes the *Who* (our target customer), the *What* (the overall marketing activity) and the *When* (the period of time). The intersection between the Who and What is the differentiation, engagement

Figure 5.3 3D go-to-market ecosystem

and influence we want to create among our potential customers as we build the relationships that are so important in B2B; the intersection of the What and When defines the programmes and campaigns we take to market; and the intersection between the Who and the When conveys the consistency and sustainability of those programmes and campaigns over time.

Once we've developed this thinking we can get into the nitty-gritty of the marketing plan.

After the strategy comes the plan: an eight-step marketing planning framework

For the bulk of my career I've used an eight-step planning model to co-create what is, in effect, marketing's contract with and accountability to the business (Figure 5.4).

These eight steps involve answering eight sets of critical questions with the business.

1 Purpose and objectives

Why are we doing this and what do we want to achieve? Are we in alignment with the business/marketing strategy?

By clearly articulating the purpose and the objectives for our marketing activity, we are able to understand and agree with the business upfront what success looks like. This not only gives us clarity on what and how we measure success but makes marketing accountable to the business for an agreed outcome.

Figure 5.4 3D marketing planning framework

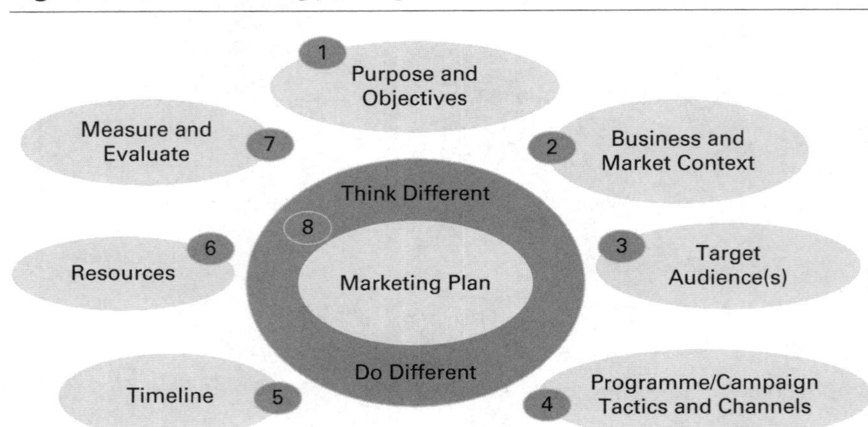

2 Business and market context

What is the environment in which we're doing business?

Developing a deep understanding of the current threats and opportunities for the business helps us to understand what is likely to change, because we know that change is inevitable. We will also be able to develop a better sense of the big issues our customers are facing.

An overview of the business climate and market outlook ensures that marketing and the business are working under the same set of assumptions. It also gives us a chance to test and double-check those assumptions through appropriate market, competitor and customer research.

3 Target audience(s)

Who will we engage with? How will we segment and select? What are their needs and issues and challenges?

In his many presentations to consumer marketing audiences, Mark Ritson often asks a question: 'How many marketers does it take to change a lightbulb?' The answer? 'Millennials'! His point is that for the B2C marketing world, every answer to the question of 'who is our target audience?' is invariably the same. Millennials, a group of people who happen to have been born between 1980 and 2000, a span of 20 years.

How many B2B marketers does it take to change a lightbulb? C-suite! Ritson's point is just as valid for B2B. We continue to focus our B2B marketing efforts on the C-suite, even though the whole point of segmentation is that we identify groups of potential customers who are all similar to each other in terms of needs, issues or challenges. We then select which segment – based on these issues and challenges – we are going to target with our marketing.

Because the sales cycle in B2B is so long and complex, we have to remember that while someone in the C-suite may have ultimate sign-off, there are many more people at all levels throughout the organization who may have a profound influence over that decision. And these people often have very different needs and challenges from those of the C-suite.

This may well be the most critical part of the planning process and we mustn't make assumptions about who our audience actually is and what their most pressing concerns are. Otherwise, all the marketing effort that follows will be either completely irrelevant or annoying or both.

4 Programme/campaign tactics and channels

What is our narrative and our core message(s)? What tactics, through which channels, and how are they interlinked?

This step in the marketing plan describes the programme or campaign we are creating. For clarity, I use the word 'campaign' to describe a shorter-term activity, with a discrete beginning and end, usually within a one-year timeframe. On the other hand, a 'programme' may well be multi-year and thematic, without a discrete end, and function as an umbrella for multiple campaigns.

It is important to reinforce here that I don't advocate delivering tactics in isolation; simply delivering a series of fragmented tactics through various channels over time does not comprise an effective marketing plan. My approach encourages developing an integrated set of programmes or campaigns that have a purpose, are targeted to a specific market and customer segment, tell a story and have a measurable outcome.

This part of the planning process formulates the tangibles that marketing will deliver and the output we are committing to; in other words, the specific tactics and channels that we will use as part of our identifiable programmes or campaigns to engage with our customers.

5 Timeline

Which activity over what period of time? How will they interlink/overlap?

The timeline is our calendar of activity and is part of our contract with the business. It should also clearly convey who is responsible for what. But we should also look at the timeline not just as a list of what's happening when; the timeline should give us a sense of how our stories are developing over time, and if there are overlapping or interlinking narratives that will provide us with other opportunities for engagement.

In addition, the timeline should include hard and soft milestones – particularly with longer programmes or campaigns – so that we (and the business) understand the commitments that will invariably be needed.

6 Resources

What resources do we need? Beyond the budget, do we have the right marketing people, structure and tools?

We now know the approach we are going to take and what we are going to do. The big question, as always, is what do we need to make it all happen? Of course, we will need a cash budget and this is where we develop our costs as well as our spending priorities.

But beyond the budget, do we have the right people with the right skills for the marketing activity we are planning? If we need capacity or specific capability for particular programmes, projects or campaigns, we may need to bring in people from other parts of our organization, or external contractors or agencies.

These resources, when combined, will determine whether we will actually be able to implement the plan.

7 Measure and evaluate

How will we measure success? Are our metrics meaningful and clear? Has the business bought into these measures?

We have already agreed with our business at the beginning of the planning process what the objectives are and what success looks like. Now we must put in place the metrics that measure the achievement of these objectives and this success. And these metrics must be specific and meaningful.

But this stage of the marketing plan isn't just about putting metrics in place.

In Chapter 4 I discussed marketing ROI in some depth, because I continue to believe that we are measuring the wrong things, just because we can. It is essential that we find ways of measuring what we do, otherwise we never really learn what works and what doesn't.

Critically, we must start taking the time to evaluate as well as measure our marketing efforts. How many of us have regular marketing debriefs, either during the course of, or at the end of, a project? Perhaps we put together a dashboard of the things we can measure and point to this as success. And then we move on.

Instead, we must first decide if what we *can* measure is meaningful to what we're trying to achieve. Then we need to take the time – again, with the business, with our salespeople – to look at what we've done so that we understand if we have achieved what was intended. There also may be varying degrees of achievement. We can ask and answer three more questions at this stage:

- What worked?
- What didn't?
- What would have been better if...?

These questions aren't about success or failure, they are about continuously learning from what we do, and becoming better marketers as a result.

Most importantly, if we plan these measures from the outset and they are understood and agreed with the business, we will never be in a position of having to 'prove' the value that marketing brings.

8 Think different, do different

Is this memorable? Does it matter to our customers?

The final element of developing the marketing plan is also an essential component to every other stage. In B2B marketing, we tend to do many of the same things in many of the same ways, year after year, because they've always (more or less) worked for us. Even though we've likely incorporated the newer tactics and channels, and adopted at least some of the newer technology into what we do, we're not fundamentally doing anything differently, we're not asking different questions, of ourselves, of our organizations or of our customers.

Part of the joy and the challenge of being a B2B marketer is that we have the opportunity to continually reinvent ourselves. Just because a generation of marketers have grown up focused on narrow skill sets and functional instead of inspirational role models doesn't mean we are no longer able to rise above the pervading 'sameness'. But it does mean we need to continually ask different kinds of questions, from the perspective of our customers, whose needs we serve, and if the answer to these questions – is this memorable? does this matter? – are negative, then we have to start thinking and doing differently with our marketing activity.

Finally, we must remember that the marketing plan is a working document and is never fixed in stone. The marketing plan must be able to flex because we can't and don't always anticipate change.

These eight steps for marketing planning aren't easy, but they do give us a planning framework and process that doesn't feel quite so complicated or overwhelming. When completed, the outcome can be rendered clearly on eight slides – or pages, whatever you prefer, as long as it's concise – that everyone can understand and align with.

Planning provides real clarity not only for marketing, but also for the business. By including them in the planning process, the business buys into marketing success. But more importantly, this model and these questions act as a catalyst for the kinds of conversations we should be having with the business so that we're able to develop and execute marketing plans that actually make a difference.

Applying 3D marketing to business strategy

Marketing isn't unique in its struggle to develop a meaningful strategy. Some of us, perhaps many of us, work in companies without a clearly articulated business strategy. Even though having a strategy is essential to the growth and sustainability of any organization, large or small, many grapple with developing, communicating and executing a meaningful strategy. When the economy is strong, this may not appear to matter, and these companies quite often muddle along profitably. Yet, as we've seen within the marketing context, strategy is a guide to the future – no matter the economic landscape – and forms the foundation and touchstone for all the myriad decisions that are made every single day across our businesses.

As we've seen, we can develop our marketing strategy effectively even if our business does not have a strategy. Yet, whether or not our organizations have a strategy, developing our own marketing strategy and plans often provides a benefit and value in and of itself to the wider business, for two very important reasons:

1. The *3D Marketing System for Strategy and Planning* is a framework that stresses interaction and collaboration with the business. It forces us out of our marketing silo and encourages us to ask the big and often hard questions about what our business wants to achieve, its priorities and needs. With an outside-in approach, we are able to ask questions about our customers that our salespeople may not even be considering. What follows is marketing activity that the business has bought into, understands and values, and sees as contributing to the bottom line.
2. This, in turn, compels our business to ask the same questions of themselves, in the context of the wider business, not just marketing. My *3D Marketing System* can just as easily be used to develop strategy and plans by and for the business. And this is the holy grail of marketing, that we are able to participate in and influence the wider business strategy.

Business strategy can be developed in exactly the same way as we've discussed above for marketing strategy. Applying 3D marketing for a business strategy encompasses the Why, Where and How for an organization, either from the ground up or to test and revise existing strategy. And we in B2B marketing are uniquely positioned to better address this with the business.

CASE STUDY A business growth strategy

The CEO of a medium-sized software company asked me to take a look at their go-to-market strategy. During the process, using my 3D Marketing System, we looked at their wider business and growth strategy, with an emphasis on articulating purpose, goals and aspirational positioning.

Early on in the day-long session the team had an 'Aha!' moment; they realized that they had been thinking about their business from the perspective of the software they sold instead of from the perspective of the customers they wanted to engage with in order to grow. In addition, for the first time, they realized that in order to achieve their growth aspirations, they needed to be service-led rather than product-led, and prioritize both their sales and marketing efforts to a completely different segment of the market.

What started out as a marketing exercise became a business exercise that fundamentally changed how they thought about their business. And by the end of the day, we had developed clarity of purpose for their organization, new customer segmentation and articulated a brand story that encompassed a distinct strategy for the future.

Doing different for B2B marketing 06

CASE STUDY Unilever's four strategic principles

I continue to believe that B2B marketing can and must learn from the B2C marketing world. For many years I have attended the Marketing Week Live conference that's held in London every spring. Many of my colleagues in B2B have tended to dismiss these types of events because they are mainly consumer focused. But as our customers in B2B continue to bring their consumer buying behaviours into our B2B world, I find that B2C marketing can and does offer us both guidance and inspiration.

I've learned a lot about marketing from Unilever over the years. In May 2015, at the Marketing Week Live conference, I listened to the then senior VP of global marketing, Marc Mathieu, speak about Unilever's marketing strategy. What I loved is that practically the first thing he said was that their strategy is not about customers, it's about *people*, with four main principles that define their strategy (and my interpretation of those principles highlighted in italics):

- **Craft brands for life** – *this is about clearly understanding and defining the brand, with trust and purpose at the core.*
- **Put people first** – *not just a customer perspective but a people perspective, it's about being HUMAN.*
- **Build brand love** – *speak to what matters, to people.*
- **Unlock the magic** – *deliver an amazing experience.*

This was truly a 'Wow' moment for me. What a simple yet compelling strategy for any era, not just the social era. This is a strategy that encompasses – as Marc phrased it – 'not just product truth, but human truth'. It's a strategy created for the long term, no matter how the business environment may change, and a strategy that all marketers within the organization can relate to, forming the foundation for every marketing activity.

Marc later left Unilever, but his legacy clearly lives on. In December 2016, Keith Weed, Chief Marketing and Communications Officer at Unilever, published two very interesting and related articles, one in *Marketing Week* online and the other on LinkedIn.

In the *Marketing Week* article, Keith wrote – and I agree – that 'despite the speed of change around us getting faster and faster, some things are an absolute analogue constant'. He went on to address three of the Unilever strategic principles from Marc's marketing strategy presentation the prior year – put people first, build brand love and unlock the magic. Yet it was how he described 'unlocking the magic' that really resonated, because he described this principle as 'connecting and building relationships' with content at the heart of those relationships. And he challenged marketers to 'connect in meaningful ways that create impact'.

In his LinkedIn post a few days later, Keith expanded on putting people first. He explained that at Unilever it means keeping people's basic needs at the heart of what they do. That even while technology transforms our world, it's important to 'remember that these are real people with real lives'.

Unilever practises what it preaches. At Cannes Lion in 2016, they launched a commitment to remove unhelpful stereotypes, particularly in relation to women, from their advertising, and they called on the industry to join them. And most of us are aware of the ongoing work they continue to do around women and body image, the Dove 'real beauty' campaign being the one that instantly springs to mind.

This speaks to the heart of issues that really matter to, and impact, their customers. And it's this relentless care for and authentic interest in these 'people' issues that engage individuals far beyond what Unilever sells.

As Keith said in his article: 'I believe that those brands who put people at the heart of their creativity and ideation will succeed more in engaging in a meaningful way with consumers, and by getting closer to the communities that our [customers] are part of we can better understand them' (*Marketing Week*, 2016).

What B2B marketers can learn from Unilever

We in B2B marketing should pay attention to these words from Unilever's CMO, because relationships remain at the heart of the B2B business environment. As I discussed in Chapter 1, our customers in B2B want to buy from people and organizations that they *like* to do business with, whose values align with their own, and with whom they feel they can build trusted, long-lasting relationships. Our marketing activity needs to reflect this long-term connection and commitment to our customers, and we mustn't take it for granted.

This is how we begin to *do different*, and this is a lesson we can and must learn in B2B marketing.

A return to marketing

Having a marketing plan is *not* the same as having a marketing strategy. Yet because we continue to equate the two, we remain stuck in doing what we've always done, believing that just because we're using the latest new channels or tactics, we are strategic. In doing so, we've lost our way, leaving behind the fundamentals that every properly trained marketing professional has learned because we've been led to believe that the technology has, in effect, made the underlying principles redundant. Thus, without a technical understanding of our discipline, we have become a profession of project managers and tactical implementers.

Isn't it time we made a return to marketing? In Part Two, I've explored in depth the four elements of brand, strategy, customers and measurement that form the foundation for marketing. These are the fundamentals of marketing, essential principles that enable us to *do different*, and without which our profession has no meaning or impact. In doing so, I've applied Simon Sinek's Golden Circle of Why, How and What to B2B marketing and suggested a shift in our B2B marketing perspective, moving from what we do (inside-out) to why it matters (outside-in).

Our Why in B2B marketing involves our brand purpose and our purpose as marketers. Our How is our marketing strategy, the approach we take to our markets, starting with our customers. Our What then becomes the activity we undertake to engage with those customers. Finally, measurement is the means through which we learn what works and what doesn't in achieving our goals and objectives, instead of a tick-box exercise to fulfil meaningless ROI criteria.

I've put a spotlight once again on yet another pervading marketing fallacy – that our marketing plans amount to our marketing strategy. I've clearly illustrated the difference between strategy and plans, and why it is imperative that strategy forms the foundation for our plans; one simply mustn't exist without the other. Yet strategy is hard and we invariably default to the plan – the execution of the tactics – because it's what we know and what we do well.

I've also explored in depth the concept of customer engagement, as opposed to the concept of customer experience, and why we mustn't confuse the two. Customer engagement is all about the ongoing interactions our customers have with our organizations, while customer experience is all about the accumulated perceptions of those interactions. The former is currently measured by marketing ROI and the latter by customer satisfaction. I've argued that B2B marketing needs to focus first on getting the customer engagement piece right before we start considering how to 'own' the entire customer experience. Which led to a look at how we measure marketing value as well as how zero-based budgeting might be a better way for us to become accountable for what we deliver for our businesses.

Finally, I've introduced my 3D Marketing System for Strategy and Planning, which provides a framework and structure for processes that are too often overwhelming, hurriedly completed or not done at all.

Essential steps to *do different*

We must *do different* if we are ever to *be different* from our competitors.

In our B2B marketing world, we tend to rely on doing the marketing activity that's always worked for us. This isn't actually surprising considering that most of our organizations are highly risk averse. So, we take last year's marketing plan and update it for the current year, perhaps adding a few new activities, doing some things slightly differently, although not essentially doing anything very different. And too often we do this without any strategy to guide our efforts.

But good enough simply isn't good enough any more. Our customers want different things from us, our businesses want different things from us. So, we need to stop relying on the marketing activity that we have always done and start asking ourselves: are we really doing the right things? And it's not just about doing the same things a bit differently; it's about doing fundamentally different things.

Like understanding our purpose, both as a business and as B2B marketers. Like developing a marketing strategy where there isn't one. Like questioning what we think we know about our customers. Like being accountable to our businesses.

Just like thinking different, doing different is not easy. It most often entails stepping out of our comfort zones and doing many things we may never have done before, which can feel risky, particularly when the outcome is uncertain. We may succeed, we may fail. And our reputations and credibility as marketers are always on the line. We are only as good as the last thing we've done.

But we will be better equipped to *do different* if we are grounded in the marketing fundamentals. If we have clarity on what our brands stand for, we have developed and agreed a marketing strategy and plans with our businesses, we deeply understand our customers and markets, and we have put in place meaningful measures for what we do, then our businesses will trust us to do what's right as well as different.

Where do we start? Five habits to nurture

As with thinking different, the first step is to make a conscious decision to fundamentally do some very different things. We can start by nurturing these five habits:

1. **Don't make assumptions** – everything changes, the market, our customers, our business needs, our priorities, ourselves. Don't assume that what was true yesterday will be true today, just because everyone in your business, department or team believes it. Challenge each and every assumption appropriately and we just might be surprised at what we discover.
2. **Cultivate curiosity** – related to the first habit above, we need to continually ask questions and really listen to the answers. The best marketers are infinitely curious. They ask questions, lots of questions, and they aren't afraid of what might be perceived as the 'stupid questions', because they really want to understand what's important and why. The ability to ask the right questions and then sit back and listen is a critical habit for marketers. And the two crucial questions can be uncomfortable to ask: Why are we doing this? Does this matter to our customers?
3. **Apply the domino effect** – start by focusing on just one thing, whether that be a single output or a specific activity for one part of your business. If you can shake up even a single way of doing something, it has the potential to spread throughout the entire organization. And you just might be surprised by who approaches you to say, 'I want one of those [marketing activities].'
4. **Create an ongoing dialogue with the business** – marketing is simply not a set of standard exercises that we do day-in and day-out, and it doesn't happen in a vacuum. We need to have conversations with our salespeople all the time so we must create the environment and the opportunity for both formal and informal discussion.
5. **Be patient** – doing different takes time, time to have the appropriate conversations, time to find the right thing, time to get business buy-in, time to plan and execute, and time to understand the results. Change is hard, and, especially in larger organizations, there may be a lot of people that we need to bring around to what we want to do.

Next steps: five questions and five actions

There are many questions we need to ask ourselves if we are to begin to *do different*, and I have explored many of them throughout Part Two. But the five questions shown in Table 6.1 are essential to start the process.

Table 6.1 Do different Q&A

Five questions to ask	Five actions to take
Is there a marketing strategy for my business that I understand (and can articulate), and to which my plans are aligned?	If you can't articulate your marketing strategy and instead point to your marketing plan, then you don't have a marketing strategy. Accepting this is your first step towards doing different. Challenge what's held up as strategy by asking Why, Where and How as framed in Chapter 5.
How do I develop my marketing strategy and plans?	If you have a strategy, review your process for developing that strategy as well as the process for building your subsequent plans. Speak to your leaders and teams as well as your stakeholders outside of marketing to agree a meaningful process that will be adopted by everyone. Use or adapt my 3D Marketing System.
What is my purpose?	Take the time to think about and understand why you do what you do, beyond earning a living. Understanding your own needs and motivations will better enable you to think as well as do different.
What can and will I do different(ly)?	No matter your level within your marketing organization, commit to finding and doing one thing differently, no matter the outcome. Be sure to agree this with your appropriate stakeholder.
Where does my marketing team physically sit within my organization?	Look at where you and your team physically sit. Many marketing teams sit in an area devoted to operations or what is often called internal services, and this may be on another floor or even in a different building from your salespeople. Do whatever is necessary to relocate where you'll be able to have ongoing, direct interaction with your salespeople (see more on this in Chapter 9 – Becoming B2B marketing leaders)

CASE STUDY Coca-Cola Content 2020 Initiative

Coca-Cola is often held up as a shining example of marketing greatness. Even though they've made some mistakes over their 125-year history (perhaps most notably changing the original soda formula to a sweeter version and introducing 'New Coke' in 1985), their marketing remains true to the fundamentals of brand, strategy and customers.

Coca-Cola was one of the first large global companies to understand the profound changes that were taking place throughout the consumer landscape in this second decade of this millennium. They had historically relied heavily on advertising and creative to drive their marketing activity through what had been until that time primarily one-way communication channels. But they recognized that their customers were increasingly accessing and consuming content in very new and different ways.

In early 2011, Jonathan Mildenhall – then Coca-Cola's Vice President of Global Advertising Strategy and Content Excellence, who would become their Senior Vice President of Integrated Marketing Content and Design Excellence in 2013 before moving on to a new role as Airbnb's CMO in 2014 – brought 40 of the organization's creative leaders from around the world to the Coca-Cola company headquarters in Atlanta, Georgia in the United States. Over one very intense week they developed what became the articulation of their creative agenda and the strategy that would underpin their marketing future – the Coca-Cola Content 2020 Initiative.

In a YouTube video interview and presentation with the Institute of Practitioners in Advertising in 2013, Mildenhall summed up the vision behind the initiative:

> Content is the substance or matter of brand engagement and brand conversation. Anything that can allow a consumer to engage with your brand or converse about your brand becomes content. So content should be wrapped around everything.

The initiative was launched on YouTube in 2012 and was brought to life with an animated whiteboard that was a captivating visual story from start to finish. As a B2B marketer, watching this 18-minute video was a defining moment for me. It was the first time I had ever seen or heard anyone articulate the purpose of marketing – engaging with customers – and their marketing strategy in such a compelling and completely captivating way.

Jargon aside, the Coca-Cola Content 2020 Initiative is essentially about the way that Coca-Cola's customers understand the role and relevance of the Coca-Cola Company brands, and the ways in which they relate to and engage with those brands. This is a critical point for 'content marketers' because Coca-Cola is not advocating replacing their traditional marketing activity, but is adding to it in a way that further builds the *relationships* between Coca-Cola and their customers.

Of particular note is the concept of 'liquid and linked' – ideas that are so compelling that they spread uncontrollably throughout the market while at the same time being aligned with Coca-Cola's business strategy and objectives, as well as their products. They also talk about storytelling as the foundation for the creation of their content and how their brand stories need to show a commitment to making the world a better place. This was years before corporate purpose came into vogue.

What B2B marketers can learn from Coca-Cola

My key takeaways for B2B marketers:

- Coca-Cola talk first about their move away from one-way broadcast to dynamic storytelling that creates engagement and delivers an integrated experience to unify customers around its brand.
- They then focus on the content elements – the compelling ideas – that underpin this engagement, which are of value, substance and significance to their customers; this content is also designed to support and align with the organization's business and marketing objectives.
- Around this content they develop conversations that are about more than insight. Coca-Cola uses the word 'provocative', which is a highly evocative, emotional and personal word, because it's these kinds of conversations that stay with our customers.

In other words, for those of us in B2B marketing, think first about the kind of engagement we want to have with our customers, and only then think about the content we need to create to deliver that engagement – content that is based on compelling ideas linked to organizational goals and that recognizes storytelling as the heart of marketing.

PART THREE
Be different

FALLACY 3

Marketing serves one core purpose, feeding sales.

Lead generation is the primary goal for 80 per cent of B2B marketers in the US and 82 per cent in the UK over the next 12 months.

CONTENT MARKETING INSTITUTE, 2017

07 What is the purpose of marketing?

In Chapter 4, I discussed purpose in the context of our wider organizations. But it is critically important for us as marketers to think about *our* purpose within those organizations as well as within our markets. Why do we do what we do? To what purpose? To what end? Who do we want to be, both as individuals and as marketers? In the same manner as our corporate purpose has the potential to differentiate our organizations in a crowded and commoditized marketplace, understanding our marketing purpose is a first step towards enabling us to *be different* in a world where so much of B2B marketing is virtually interchangeable.

The past decade has been rough on us in B2B marketing. Before 2008 we had been experiencing well over a decade of economic prosperity. This meant we mostly received the budgets we asked for and we had the freedom to spend without the kind of scrutiny we have today. I personally knew marketers who didn't even track marketing spend, and if they went over budget, no one seemed to care. Our businesses were receiving more or less what they expected from marketing, which mostly revolved around events, PR and brochure-ware. Let's face it, marketing got lazy; we continued to do what we'd always done and continued to be what we'd always been for our organizations. Few of us ever anticipated what was coming.

The global recession of 2008 marked the end of an era and a turning point for most of us. Alongside sluggish economic growth, technology forever and fundamentally altered the commercial landscape. We have struggled to cope with this unprecedented pace of change; even a decade later, we are still struggling. As a result, many would argue that we have lost credibility within our organizations, though I would question how much credibility we ever really had. How often do we now hear marketing referred to as 'the colouring-in department'? How many of us continue to be regarded as servants instead of partners to the business?

So, who are we and what is our purpose in the context of our times?

Let's talk about lead generation

As I was exploring purpose in the context of marketing, I had discussions with a lot of very senior marketing people, but one discussion in particular has stuck in my mind because it echoed a theme that was returned to again and again. This senior marketer told me that marketing's core purpose is to generate leads – 'marketing serves one core purpose, feeding sales'. That it's only through this lead generation activity that marketing can gain the respect of the business and be in a position to influence wider strategy.

Granted, they made some valid points – including that we waste a lot of time and money on ineffective activity, and we need to focus on delivering results for the business – yet those results are not always about leads. So, I cannot agree that 'generating leads' is the real purpose of marketing.

For clarity, I define lead generation as the marketing activity that stimulates and captures interest in a product or service in order to develop and fill the sales pipeline, with the ultimate goal being an actual sale. It is the process of identifying specific, named contacts who may be ready to buy, and one of marketing's many responsibilities is to implement activity that will capture those names to send along to sales.

Make no mistake, lead generation is not a strategic activity. It is a short-term, tactical activity, designed to do one thing and one thing only, create a never-ending pipeline of leads that sales can use to drive revenue. In the old days (pre-digital), we measured leads by the number of business cards we collected at events, and our marketing activity was designed to drive people to our stands, presentations or seminars. Other leads were generated by the number of people who signed up for our mailing lists, who were interested enough to receive ongoing communications and other marketing materials from us. Perhaps we did some advertising in trade publications, with a call to action that would identify a lead. Unless we were meticulous about following up with our salespeople and keeping our spreadsheets up to date, we had few – and often inaccurate – ways of measuring whether any of these leads were followed up and closed by sales. I have to admit that for much of my career my marketing KPIs were based on the number of names that marketing added to the contact lists or rather 'fuzzy' objectives that had to do with marketing outputs and nothing to do with revenue.

The holy grail for marketing is, of course, the measurement of marketing's contribution to revenue. This is much easier to do in the B2C world where, for example, a sale can be directly measured as revenue from a point-of-sale merchandising unit or from the uplift in sales following a specific advertising campaign. For B2B, marketing's contribution to revenue has traditionally been measured anecdotally at best, or not at all.

Today, of course, we have all sorts of tools that purport to measure marketing ROI as a function of revenue. And we should measure what we can, but with a caveat – just because we *can* measure something doesn't make it meaningful.

The Content Marketing Institute's 2017 benchmarking survey found that lead generation is the primary goal for the vast majority of B2B marketers (80 per cent of US B2B marketers and 82 per cent of UK B2B marketers). Furthermore, these marketers plan to measure the results of this lead generation through the traffic to their website (70 per cent US and 78 per cent UK). These are huge percentages of marketers who are relying upon a single channel to measure marketing's impact on sales. Yet the reality is that few, if any, B2B buyers purchase as a result of a website visit. According to Marketo, 96 per cent of B2B website visitors are not even ready to buy. They are, however, often willing to exchange their contact details for relevant, interesting content. Does this constitute a lead? For too many of us, it does indeed.

Search is a powerful tool for our customers; common wisdom has it that 80 per cent or more of our customers start their buying journey with a web search. Yet being dependent upon our website as our primary lead generation tool or the primary measure for marketing's wider lead generation activity is too simplistic and limiting. Our customers use a variety of channels to interact with our organizations and in B2B a website visit has often first been cultivated through another source. We also have no insight into the multitude of other dimensions that influence our customers' buying decisions over time.

We simply must start questioning whether we are in fact contributing in a meaningful way to our business through our lead generation activity. Is what we're measuring actually contributing to the bottom line or is it yet another numbers exercise? Digital Stream Media contends that 73 per cent of all B2B leads are not sales-ready. Furthermore, according to Mike Weir, Vertical Director for LinkedIn Marketing Solutions' Technology business, 'upwards of 80 per cent of leads generated by marketing are neglected or never acted upon by a sales rep'.

The three stonecutters revisited

In Chapter 5 I told the story of the three stonecutters. As a reminder:

- The first stonecutter was focused simply on the completion of the task and the quantity of output.

- The second stonecutter was also focused on the amount of output, but with a quality dimension as compared to other stonecutters.
- However, the third stonecutter saw beyond the task to what was being built, understanding the specific contribution to a larger outcome, a higher purpose.

In the context of the three stonecutters, lead generation can then be understood as a task fulfilled by the first two stonecutters – finding and shaping the stones to hand off to the builders who will then fulfil the architect's vision. This is a short-term activity, designed to meet quantity and quality quotas and standards – the builders need a certain number of stones, of a specified standard, in order to meet the requirements as directed by the architect.

Yet the third stonecutter sees and understands the future that is being built, maintaining a focus on what is being achieved by their individual efforts. This is the clarity each of us – as individuals and as marketers – needs to define and articulate for ourselves as builders and architects of that business landscape.

Are we building a cathedral or are we fashioning stones? We must begin to have different kinds of conversations with our businesses about what marketing should be achieving for the business, in terms of the organization's longer-term goals and objectives, not just in terms of short-term revenue generation. As I argued in Chapter 4, we must fundamentally reset the 'value' agenda.

I'm not saying that generating leads is unimportant; of course it's important. At the risk of oversimplifying, our organizations stay in business by acquiring customers and making money. But acquiring customers is a process – often a complex and lengthy one in B2B, with many people involved in the decision-making process. Lead generation is only one aspect of marketing. The fact that we may have better tools to measure the effectiveness of our lead generation activity than we may do for other marketing activity does not mean we should be distracted or ignore those other things which are also marketing's responsibility – namely strategy, segmentation, positioning, brand awareness, customer insight and engagement – and which enable the long-term sustainability of our companies.

We do a disservice to marketing as a function and a profession – as well as to the companies we work for – if we define ourselves solely by our tasks and short-term tactical marketing activity without a clearer understanding of our wider role and purpose as marketers.

Is marketing's purpose the generation of leads? Certainly, that is one of marketing's objectives and tasks… but its core purpose? Surely not.

A threefold purpose for marketing

The dictionary defines purpose as: 'the reason for which something is done or created or *for which something exists*' (emphasis is mine).

What is the purpose of marketing? Ask a roomful of marketers and I'm certain there will be a roomful of answers; ask 100 people across our organizations and there will be a further 100 different responses and perspectives. In addition to lead generation, just a few of the responses to this question tend to be: get the company's name out in the marketplace and create awareness of the brand; build credibility for the brand; position the brand and its products and services against competitors; and drive sales. These answers are all partially right; they're all a result of what happens if we are doing our marketing job well. I've also been told that marketing's purpose is to: create brochures; manage events; update the website; do surveys; and keep the customer lists. Again, these answers are all partially right in that these are some of the tasks that marketing does. Yet, in B2B in particular, there is a real lack of understanding about what marketing can and should actually be achieving.

I have really struggled with articulating marketing purpose over the years, but I've come to believe that marketing actually has threefold, interrelated purpose:

1. **Build, maintain and protect the brand:** this is about the awareness and credibility of our brands and how trusted we are in the marketplace. And it's not about the products or services we sell, but about our organizations – who we are, why we do what we do, and how we do it.
2. **Customer engagement:** engaging our customers – attracting, appealing to, pleasing, connecting with and retaining our customers using the appropriate tools, channels and technology at our disposal – remains the essence of marketing. In today's world, marketing has a much larger part to play than ever before; our customers are moving much further through the sales 'pipeline' without even talking to a salesperson. In fact, our customers tell us they don't want to be 'sold to' any more; so, we have to completely change our perspective and think more about how we can engage with our customers *before* their buying journey even begins. By making this our starting point, we are able to better understand our customers and connect through what they really care about, what matters to them, what challenges they deal with every day, and what really drives their buying decisions (and it's not bigger, better, faster, cheaper any more).

3 **Drive demand:** this is not the same as generating leads, though leads are a natural outcome of the process. Because while lead generation is the short-term process of identifying specific contacts which may result in a sale, demand generation requires a longer-term, far wider, more holistic marketing approach that builds awareness and interest and creates engagement around customer issues, while aligning with what we sell.

Of course, how we do all this depends upon our business and our marketing strategy. And it takes an unrelenting, long-term commitment. But, taken together, these three elements *create the environment* in which we can more effectively achieve our organization's strategic goals and objectives; in other words, an environment in which we can do better business. And perhaps this is how to articulate our purpose as marketers: that we exist *to create the environment in which our organizations are better able to engage with customers to conduct business.*

Revisiting the marketing mix

In Chapter 4, I discussed the four fundamentals of marketing – brand, strategy, customers and measurement – as the necessary foundation for coming out of our tactical silos and changing 'what we do' so that we can be different with our B2B marketing activity.

Understanding the basic concept of the marketing mix and its associated 4Ps remains essential for marketing. These 4Ps are the fundamental tenets of classical marketing theory. The origin of the marketing mix concept itself has been attributed to Professor John Culliton, who colourfully described marketers as 'artists' and 'mixers of ingredients' in a 1948 *Harvard University Research Bulletin* (Borden, 1964):

> … who sometimes follows a recipe prepared by others, sometimes prepares his own recipe as he goes along, sometimes adapts a recipe to the ingredients immediately available, and sometimes experiments with or invents ingredients no one else has tried.

What *no one else has tried…* this from the 1940s no less! This is the essence of being different and I would argue that it remains a key ingredient for the entire marketing mix.

The 4Ps were formally first introduced in the 1960s by marketer and academic E Jerome McCarthy in his textbook *Basic Marketing: A managerial approach*, although fellow professor Neil Borden takes credit for coining the term in the late 1950s. It has since become one of the most enduring and widely accepted frameworks in marketing.

The marketing mix is commonly defined as the set of actions and tools that a company has control over and undertakes or uses in order to strengthen its brand and sell its products or services. For the B2B marketer of today, I define the *marketing mix* more simply as the integrated combination of marketing tools and tactics that that we use to engage our customers.

We all know (or should know) the 4Ps (Figure 7.1).

We don't often think much about the 4Ps – even during our marketing strategy and planning process – because it's one of those concepts that 'everyone knows' and as such doesn't seem to be considered as even a basic knowledge requirement any more. Furthermore, as our commercial landscape has increased in complexity, there have been extensions to these 4Ps so that we now have the 7Ps for services marketing and the 4Cs for what is known as the customer-focused marketing mix (Figure 7.2).

There is an argument that the 4Ps are outdated and were more useful in the early part of the last century when manufacturing and physical products dominated our commercial landscape. We can debate whether or not the later iterations are more useful in our service-dominated and customer-focused era of marketing or if they are simply using more contemporary language to

Figure 7.1 The 4Ps of the marketing mix

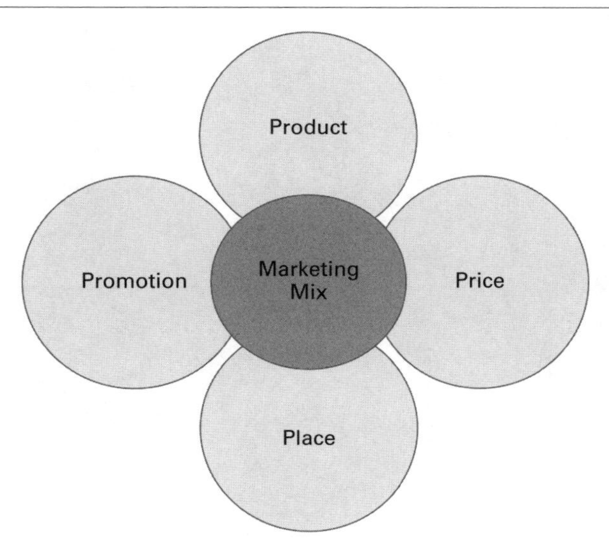

Figure 7.2 The 7Ps of the services marketing mix and the 4Cs of the customer-focused marketing mix

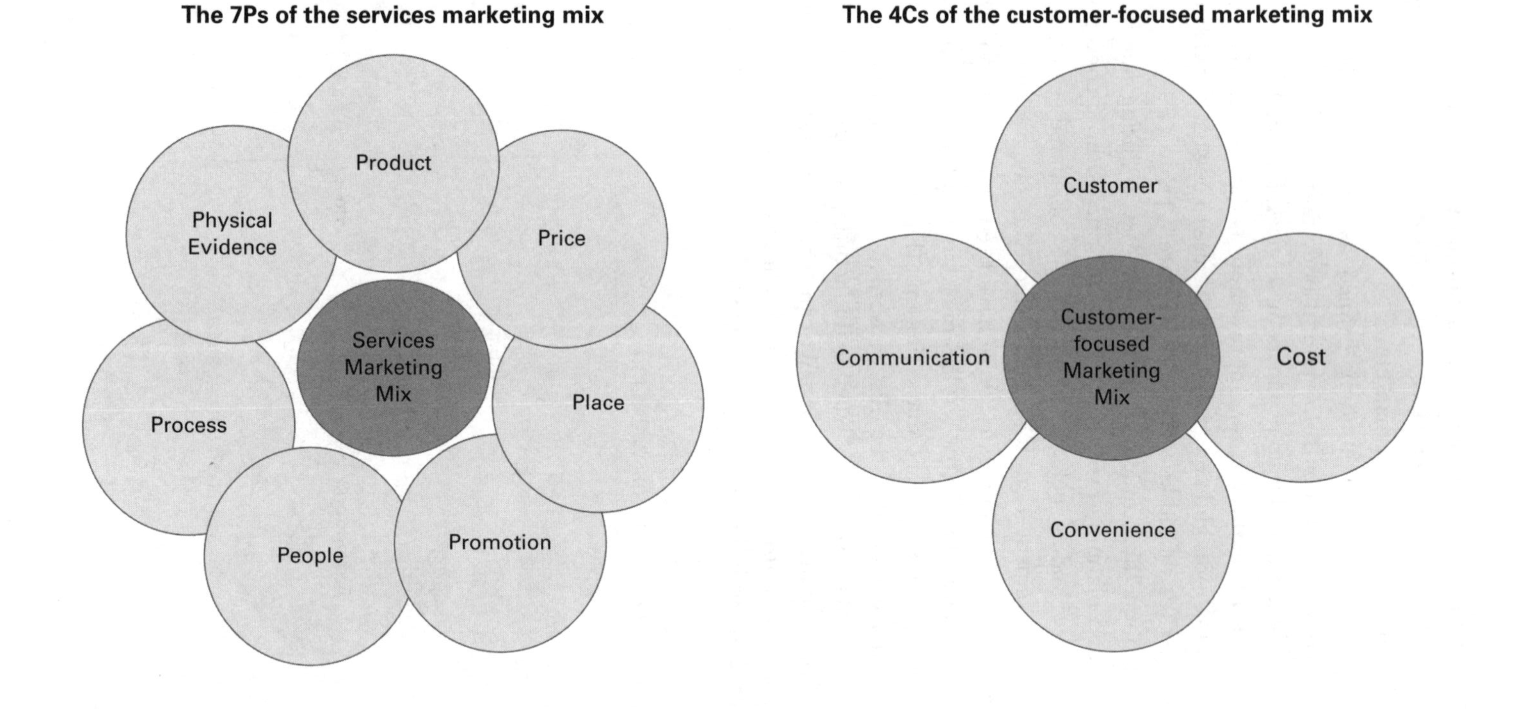

discuss the same principles. No matter which we may use, they remain useful models for considering what we do, and how and why we do it.

Let's look more closely at the 4Ps, 7Ps and 4Cs models.

The 4Ps of the marketing mix

McCarthy's 4Ps model is traditionally described as:

1. **Product**: The first of the 4Ps is product. A product fulfils a need or provides a solution to a problem or challenge for a customer, and it can be either a tangible good or an intangible service. No matter whether we sell a physical product that we can see and touch or whether we sell our skills and expertise in areas such as banking, finance, insurance, consulting, IT or tax, among others, it's imperative that we understand exactly what our product is, the need it fills, and what makes it different from our competitors' products. This is our product or service offering, and, in B2B, marketing's role is typically in the development of the product's value proposition and its routes to market, not the product or service itself.
2. **Price**: Once we understand our product or service, and where it sits within our competitor landscape, we can make pricing decisions based on required profit margins, supply and demand in the marketplace, and both business and marketing strategy. In B2B, marketing isn't often involved in pricing discussions (perhaps we should be asking ourselves, 'why not?') but it's critical to understand the pricing issues in our markets. For example, if we are a premium-priced supplier, are we communicating that extra value to our customers?
3. **Place**: We often hear that marketing is about putting the right product, at the right price, in the right place, at the right time. Place is thus about channel choice, where we distribute, position and sell our products, as well as engage and interact with our customers. In the context of B2B marketing, our emphasis is less on product or service distribution and sales, and more on the channels we use to engage with our customers before, during and after the buying process.
4. **Promotion**: Promotion is the final element of the 4Ps model and it is where marketing is becoming stuck. This is the purely tactical element of the 4Ps model and is intended to create differentiation and generate demand for our products or services. It also encompasses the way we communicate with all of our stakeholders, both internal and external, about our organization as well as about what we sell.

The 7Ps of the services marketing mix

The 7Ps model, also known as the services marketing mix or 7Ps of Booms and Bitner, is an extension of McCarthy's 4Ps model introduced in 1981 by Bernard H Booms and Mary J Bitner, both academics and researchers in the field of services management and services marketing. The 7Ps added three new elements to the 4Ps model in order to better describe the marketing mix as the services sector began to dominate many economies.

These additional Ps can be helpful because even though they are most often described in business management terms, they do provide further insight and direction for marketers, which I have added to the more common descriptions.

5 **People:** The services sector is more reliant on the human element than the manufacturing sector. A service 'product' is invariably dependent upon the capability, knowledge and skills of the people who deliver that service. This element of the 7Ps is intended to reflect the importance of all of the people throughout an organization in the ultimate delivery of that service. However, this People element should also refer to the people more widely across our organization and the people we sell to. From a marketing perspective, this element helps us consider how we may best market our organization's expertise, in other words, our people, and reminds us that we also need to understand the people we do business with. This fifth P should encompass market and customer research, segmentation and targeting.

6 **Processes:** The resources, support systems and processes within an organization directly impact the ability of that organization to deliver a service. This includes marketing. What do we need in terms of human and financial resources? What capabilities and skills do we need for our marketing teams? Do we have the right support systems and technology?

7 **Physical evidence:** Because services are made tangible only once they are delivered, physical evidence most often refers to the evidence that demonstrates the value of the service or confirms the standards or conditions for successful service delivery. But it has also come to mean the physical manifestation of an organization's presence in the marketplace, such as its actual buildings or its brand perception. For marketing, this element is about providing evidence for what the customer is buying, which in a services business is most often about buyer perceptions; this activity is also tactical in nature.

We can each decide for ourselves whether the 4Ps or the 7Ps are more useful to us in our specific marketing roles. But the marketing mix and these models remain a worthwhile tool for us to examine the combination of factors that we as marketers can control to influence the buying decision. It's also an important reminder for us – promotion alone isn't enough; there are an awful lot of factors that contribute to business success or failure. Our marketing decisions are affected by, and should therefore be aligned with, other functional areas within our companies.

The 4Cs for customer perspective

In 1990, Robert F Lauterborn developed the 4Cs model for the marketing mix – Customer, Cost, Convenience and Communication. Lauterborn is a professor at the University of North Carolina at Chapel Hill in the United States, and is perhaps best known as one of the pioneers of integrated marketing communications. In an *Advertising Age* article in 1990, Lauterborn argued that McCarthy's 4Ps of the 1960s were outdated, that they were created for a very different world – a world that was geared towards mass production of goods and a consumption culture where buyers behaved predictably in a linear manner in response to marketing and advertising stimuli. Although Lauterborn's model is intended as a consumer model, it works nicely within the context of B2B to help us shift our perspective from what we sell to what matters to our customers.

1 **Customer** replaces Product. The post-Second World War boom mentality of 'make it and they will buy' no longer applies to our modern business world. 'You can only sell what someone specifically wants to buy'; in other words, we must know our customers as well as, or better than, we know our products or services so that we are able to solve our customers' wants, needs and challenges.
2 **Cost** replaces Price. Price has become increasingly irrelevant as our products and services have commoditized. Bigger, better, faster, cheaper are no longer compelling enough reasons for our customers to buy from us. They can just as easily buy the same, or similar, products or services from our competitors, at the same or similar prices. Lauterborn rightly argues that there are costs other than price for the purchaser, and this is a complex balance that is different for each buyer. Cost helps us to understand the motivations behind our customers' buying decisions.
3 **Convenience** replaces Place. Lauterborn was writing about consumers at the dawn of the 1990s and was arguing that consumers no longer needed to go to a physical place in order to make a purchase. But Convenience is just as apt today in B2B because there are so many channels our customers use during their buying journey, and they move among those channels

seamlessly, according to what is most accessible and easiest at the time or place they happen to be.

4 **Communication** replaces Promotion. Our customers are no longer passive recipients of our marketing messages and they no longer behave or buy in predictable ways. Communication is about developing a dynamic, not static, dialogue with our customers so that we influence instead of manipulate. Promotion implies a perspective from the point of view of what we sell; communication implies a point of view from the customer perspective.

Reinterpreting the 4Ps for B2B marketing

The 4Ps, 7Ps and 4Cs models for developing the marketing mix have all helped to inform my thinking and doing throughout my B2B marketing career. But as I've been considering how we can be different in B2B in an environment that is no longer the same as either McCarthy's or Lauterborn's, I've reinterpreted the 4Ps for B2B in a slightly different way (Figure 7.3).

1 **People** instead of Product or Customers

Even in B2B we build brand loyalty and advocacy through human interaction and emotional engagement. Thinking about people as merely customers or potential customers keeps our focus on what we sell (our products or

Figure 7.3 The 4Ps for B2B marketing

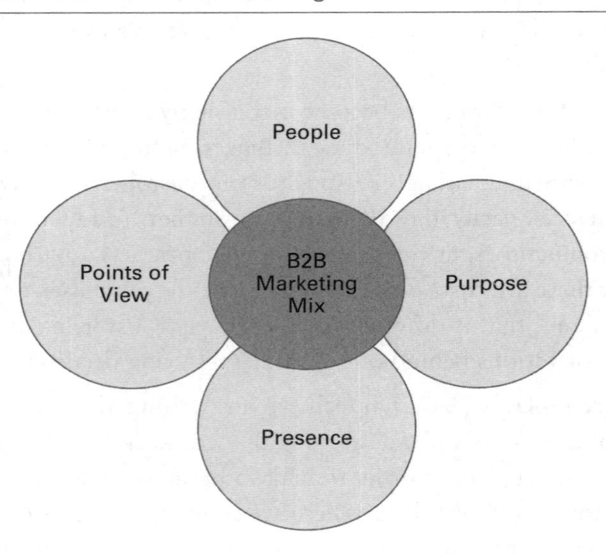

services, to our customers) instead of really getting to grips with what's important and meaningful to the people we sell to. Our customers don't magically transform from people into a job title once they're at work. Having a People perspective, not just a customer perspective, enables us to better connect with our customers and understand what really matters to them.

We also need to consider the people within our organizations, and there are a number of layers to take into account. First, especially in services companies, our people may well be the only differentiator we have from our competitors – their ideas and how they think, as well as their experience, expertise and skills. Second, our employees at all levels throughout the organization are often our greatest advocates, and in this social era their voices are heard more widely than ever before.

Finally, individual relationships are more important in B2B than in B2C. Not only is the buying cycle much longer in B2B, but delivery is often in terms of solutions that result in 'engagements' over long periods of time. Maintaining those relationships over time is just as, or even more, important than building the initial relationships that are critical in a B2B sales environment.

2 **Purpose** instead of Price or Cost

I've discussed purpose at length in Chapter 4. Corporate purpose is not just the words on the 'About Us' page of our company's website, and it's not a mission, vision or values statement; it's about what our organization stands for at a very fundamental, human level.

Rosabeth Moss Kanter, a professor at Harvard Business School and Chair and Director of the Harvard University Advanced Leadership Initiative, has said, 'The companies that perform best over time build a social purpose into their operations that is as important as their economic purpose' (*Harvard Business Review*, November 2011).

Our customers are increasingly concerned about the kinds of companies that they buy from and do business with. So, we must think not only about profits, but about the type of business we want to be in the context of the world and the society we live in. As marketers, we must work with our businesses to articulate this purpose in a way that is meaningful to our customers and authentic to our organizations.

Beyond this corporate or organizational purpose, however, we must also consider our purpose as marketers for our organizations. Just like the organizations of which we are a part, our purpose as marketers goes beyond what we do to the kinds of marketers we want to be.

3 **Presence** instead of Place or Convenience

Presence is about more than channel choice, it's about consistency, and is the authority and authenticity we project into the market as well as within our organizations. Presence is a combination of all 4Ps – a clear purpose with a meaningful and relevant point of view or proposition from a people perspective that becomes the undercurrent to everyday interactions in our markets.

Of course, that's easier said than done in the B2B world, and we need to get far better at articulating and telling a consistent story over time that's not overtly about what we sell. In this way, our customers, the people who buy our B2B products and services, understand the role and relevance of what we do to what they do.

4 **Point of View/Proposition** instead of Promotion or Communication

As B2B marketers, we are constantly challenged with being different from our competitors and telling a story that's distinctive in what is invariably a crowded marketplace. And there are broadly two types of stories we tell: the stories that have to do with our points of view (our thought leadership) and the stories that have to do with our propositions (what we sell – our brand, business, and product or service).

Thought leadership has become a staple of B2B business and we all use it to some extent as part of our marketing portfolio. Unfortunately, though, much of our thought leadership actually isn't; we don't do enough work to challenge the status quo or provide new insight into what really matters to our customers. We end up expressing an opinion, talking about the issues or providing commentary on what *is*, usually from our own singular point of view, without providing any answers on what *could be*, from our customers' perspective, or suggesting actions that might achieve a future, desired result.

Furthermore, our propositions all tend to sound the same as our competitors'; we use the same terminology, in the same ways, describing who we are or what we do in terms of ourselves – our company or our business – instead of being framed from the perspective of the customer.

Marketing as a dance – the technique underpins the story

I've spent a lot of time on the marketing mix, the 4Ps and their variations because an awful lot of us simply don't have the grounding in marketing theory and technique. No matter if you subscribe to the original 4Ps, the

7Ps, the 4Cs, my own reinterpretation of the 4Ps or a combination of all of them, my point is that we need to return to the marketing rigour that is critical to our profession.

The 4Ps remain our backbone as marketers. No single component of the marketing mix determines success, but these are the technical elements that underpin our profession, and without them we simply won't be as effective at telling our stories and connecting with our customers.

What does a ballerina have to do with B2B marketing?

In the autumn of 2016, Darcey Bussell – former Royal Ballet prima ballerina (and *Strictly Come Dancing* judge) – appeared on the Jonathan Ross Show and told a story about the advice she once received from a dance legend. She was on the show promoting a documentary about Dame Margot Fonteyn, the prima ballerina who became synonymous with English ballet and who almost single-handedly propelled the Royal Ballet and its English style onto the international stage.

The story Darcey told was this: At the age of 20, she was about to perform her first *Swan Lake* as prima ballerina. At the time, Darcey was obsessed with technique, with the execution of the dance steps – sustaining the *en pointe*, the positioning of her arms, the height of her leaps and so on. During rehearsals, she met and was mentored by Dame Margot, who told her that she had mastered the technical elements of the dance so was now able to concentrate on the story, that all her years of training meant she could forget about the technique and focus on the performance in order to connect with her audience.

I use this story a lot as an analogy for B2B marketing. It's interesting that Darcey became such a renowned ballerina precisely because of her tremendous technical ability; this technique formed the foundation for everything that came afterwards and enabled her to develop her own special lyricism that connected her with her audiences and differentiated her from other ballerinas of her time.

This is Darcey's lesson for B2B marketers: learn the technique and learn it well; once we learn the basics we can move on to attempt the special, the breath-taking, the singular that will make an impact different from any other. Further, technique and storytelling work together; unless the technique is superb, the story cannot be told as effectively. In other words, without the foundation – the technique, the theory and the understanding of the dance itself – it is impossible to interpret the story through the medium in a way that really matters to the audience.

Marketing is like a dance. We absolutely must get the steps right and we must do them well, linking those steps seamlessly, so we are able to engage and connect effectively with our customers. Otherwise marketing becomes just a lot of fancy footwork without any relevance or meaning at all.

4Cs for B2B marketing – Clarity, Credibility, Consistency and Competitiveness

I can just hear the groans, not another model! But I have another important point to make. An awful lot of our B2B marketing activity takes place in Lauterborn's Communications sphere, which I've extended to include developing our Points of View and our Propositions.

The 4Cs for marketing communications (Clarity, Credibility, Consistency, Competitiveness) were created by David Jobber and John Fahy and introduced in their book *Foundations of Marketing* (McGraw-Hill, 2003). While the 4Cs generally refer to the Lauterborn model I discussed earlier, these 4Cs are incredibly useful reminders when positioning our businesses, creating our thought leadership and developing our brand, business, product or service value propositions:

- **clarity**: a distinct idea, story or message, simply stated;
- **credibility**: the idea, story or message must be relevant, authentic and trusted;
- **consistency**: the same idea, story or message told again and again, by the entire organization, over time;
- **competitiveness**: differentiated from your competitors, appealing to your customers.

Way back in 2013, CEB and Google were telling us that 86 per cent of B2B buyers saw 'no real difference between suppliers' (CEB and Google, 2013). This wasn't a surprise to me; for years I had been doing customer research that continually told me our B2B customers saw nothing to differentiate the key players in my industry. Yet our value propositions more or less followed the same template:

> **[The world/business]** is changing. **[Customers/employees]** are demanding **[more/less]** of **[something]**. That's why **[we]** have a new approach. We've created a **[dynamic/innovative/unique]** model that combines **[solutions/partners/propositions]** and that truly **[empowers/enables/reimagines]** your **[people/customers/business]** to deliver more **[productivity/sales/efficiency/great customer experience]** and less **[cost/time to market]**.
> (The Marketing Practice, CXcellence, November 2016)

Most thought leadership simply isn't. Our value propositions are all the same. We go to market in the same ways. How, then, can we be different?

Not enough C-words: the dearth of creativity in B2B

Is marketing art or science? Incredibly, this debate is not new; it has been raging for more than 70 years, ever since Paul D Converse, an American economist and marketing professor at the University of Illinois, published a paper titled 'The development of the science of marketing: an exploratory survey'(*Journal of Marketing*, 1945).

Yet this debate is perhaps more important now than ever before. The proliferation of digital channels has brought an abundance of tools and technologies that enable us to extract all sorts of data about our markets and customers from those channels. This has brought real challenges for marketers. There is so much data out there and we don't have the time or, some would say, the skills to interpret that data and turn it into the information and insight that can form the foundation for our marketing decisions.

As we've narrowed our marketing focus on digital, we've become ever further removed from our customers, not closer to them. We may have more data available to us – about our customers' buying habits, their lifestyles, their issues, their wants and needs – yet because we are so focused on making sense of all this customer data we've become too reliant on it. Where is the human being in the data? Our customers are not a number in our CRM systems, to be scored, analysed, sent along to the sales department (or not) and then included (or not) in our next digital communication.

Data, if interpreted correctly, may tell us what customers do, but it doesn't tell us why. Data may inform our marketing activity, but it doesn't necessarily drive the kind of results marketing must deliver on a sustainable basis for the long term.

Art or science? If the science is in the data, then the art is in everything else.

C is for Creativity

I often worry that the bulk of marketing talent goes into the consumer or agency world, because B2B is perceived as not being cool or creative. Furthermore, we have become overly focused on the data skills gap in our organizations because we've been led to believe that 'the answers' are in the data. As a result, B2B marketing seems to have become focused almost exclusively on the science. I've even had senior marketing directors tell me that marketing is *all* about the data and they are prioritizing bringing more data analysts into their marketing teams.

I'm concerned about the data, too, but mostly because we can make it mean just about anything we want it to mean. Time and again, without even intending to, I see 'data' used to validate what we think we already know, or to prove a particular point of view.

However, I'm much more concerned about the almost total lack of creativity within many B2B marketing organizations and the dearth of creative thinking among a large proportion of marketing B2B leaders. Just think about the marketing that has stood out over the past few years. What has made it distinctive? Not the data, certainly. As one inspired marketing director I know said to me: 'Creativity still beats everything else – whether that's being creative with creative or creative with the approach.'

We don't see a lot of real creativity within any part of B2B. There are notable exceptions, though.

Not 'boring' B2B: three inspiring B2B case studies

CASE STUDY Schneider Electric

Schneider Electric is a global specialist in energy management and automation for both the consumer and B2B markets. They've done some wonderful work within their 'Life Is On' campaign which utilizes both 'new' and traditional marketing tactics, including YouTube video, print, online and out-of-home advertising, e-mail, corporate website, and events with a focus on their core themes of sustainability and efficiency.

My favourite of their B2B targeted videos is the 'Llama Superstar'. A bored facilities manager who sits in a windowless room doesn't think the job is all that important. While at the photocopier, the air conditioning system in the building goes down and the facilities manager receives an alert via smartphone. At the same time, in a stuffy boardroom, an overheated executive is hesitating over signing a large communications contract while the sales team nervously looks on and sweats. The facilities manager resets the air conditioning, the contract is signed, a communications satellite is launched and internet access is brought to a remote mountain top in Peru where a little girl dreams of a pony. Her father films their llama playing a musical instrument, uploads to the internet, the video goes viral and he earns a huge cheque that enables him to buy a pony for his daughter. All thanks to the facilities manager, who now feels like a hero.

It's an amusing and entertaining backdrop for what are often considered 'boring' B2B products and services.

CASE STUDY IBM

IBM is another company that illustrates the power of creativity in B2B. They may not have the flashiness of a Google or an Apple, yet they consistently deliver powerful 'big idea' marketing activity. They were one of the first to recognize the power of technology with their Smarter Planet brand strategy, which spanned seven years, and included spin-offs such as their Smarter Cities initiative. In 2015, they made a wholesale change to the way they frame their business both internally and externally by replacing their Smarter Planet brand strategy with what they call Cognitive Business, promoted by their Watson technology. This is only the third update of their brand platform in the past 20 years and reflects the fact that 'digital' is no longer a key differentiator for brands but an integral part of our world.

B2B marketers take note: IBM launched Cognitive Business with so-called traditional marketing tactics such as print inserts and television spots, complemented by outdoor display advertising, as well as paid search and social media.

IBM also did a wonderful campaign celebrating their centennial in 2011 with a YouTube film that paired stories of the 100 years of IBM history with people who were born in that year. What made this film so special was that it brought to life the human element of the IBM story.

Similarly, the marketing team leveraged their history in the 2013 '60 Years in Singapore' campaign. They paired stories of IBM's 60 years of operation in Singapore with an imagining of 60 years into Singapore's future and shared the stories of real people.

Here is a giant of a company that's been quietly going about its business for over 100 years, continually reinventing itself without veering from its roots, and creating memorable marketing moments consistently over time. Remember in the

1990s IBM's Big Blue became the first machine to play and win a chess match – beating Garry Kasparov, then reigning world champion? Or IBM's Watson winning the US game show *Jeopardy!* in 2011 against two former champions?

These are marketing moments that linger and illustrate how even staid brands can make an impact long after that moment is over.

CASE STUDY Berwin Leighton Paisner

International law firm Berwin Leighton Paisner (BLP) is embracing creativity at the heart of their B2B marketing activity. The legal sector is notoriously risk averse yet highly competitive, with often dozens of reputable firms competing for major business mandates. That competition creates a lot of choice for BLP's customers – in-house counsel and business leaders within major financial institutions, investors and corporations – but it also creates lots of noise in the market with an endless sea of thought leadership, educational seminars and corporate hospitality. Standing out from the competitive crowd and winning the battle for share of voice in a marketing-wary and risk-averse industry is a continuing challenge for BLP and other law-firm marketing departments.

But BLP also has a reputation for innovation that has provided creative licence for BLP's marketing team to break new ground. They made two simple but immense leaps in their marketing thinking: they realized they needed to dare to be different in order to stand out from the crowd; and, most importantly, that their target audience, despite a reputation for risk aversion, were just regular people. Though constantly under time and other pressures, BLP's clients were ultra-bright, with a strong intellectual curiosity and an equivalently strong sense of wit.

To tap into that innate curiosity and sense of humour, BLP set out to reinvent the delivery of legal thought leadership and supporting educational seminars. Their creative twist on the tried and tested legal marketing formula was to create amusing stories to dramatize the often very serious legal issues facing clients. BLP's team then brought those stories to life using immersive experiential techniques. Brian Macreadie, Head of Brand and Campaign Marketing at BLP, provided an example of that in practice:

> Listening to our clients, we learned that some of them were haunted by past decisions made by their companies. Past decisions can develop into future nightmares so, to tackle those nightmares, we crafted the fictitious story of a (haunted) hotel business facing

> a host of shocking legal problems that our clients might face in the real world. Clients attended a seminar where our experts presented solutions to those problems, but the seminar had a twist. We haunted the event venue with, among other tongue-in-cheek shenanigans, the sordid legal problems projected as ghostly holograms, ghosts grabbing attendees through a fake wall, a horror movie teaser video and a number of visual references to famous ghost movies. It could have gone wrong, but our bravery paid off. The oversubscribed event series got hundreds of glowing testimonials, guests reported 100 per cent satisfaction and we earned multiple new business opportunities shortly after the event. A similar recent event generated a 100 per cent ROI within four weeks.

That example is just one of a series of creative showpieces that BLP's marketing team continues to experiment with. Over recent years the firm's marketing activities have involved interactive video games, sound showers, 3D light shows and heist-themed case study videos, which have all contributed to significantly increased event attendance and content readership, thousands of new business contacts and measurable improvements in brand sentiment. Ash Coleman-Smith, Marketing Director at BLP said:

> Creativity is a great source of competitive advantage for BLP, and has proven to generate a highly positive response from our clients. It generates sales and reinforces our position as a game-changer. One of my core responsibilities as marketing director is to foster a working culture within Marketing where our team is encouraged to push boundaries and feels not only safe to try new ideas, but is rewarded for doing so. And we have seen the commercial benefits of that.

Brian supported that view: 'I'm in the enviable position of having *creativity* as one of my annual performance measures, which I think is critical, alongside other, harder metrics. Standing out from the crowd requires new, braver thinking – and creativity is at the heart of that.'

Rediscovering our creativity

Energy, information technology and the legal sectors; these three sectors are often perceived as 'boring B2B', yet the case studies above demonstrate that creativity can be compelling. In fact, we'd be hard-pressed to find, in any sector, memorable brands that do not have creativity at their core. B2B marketing is only boring if we allow it to be. Creativity is not only for the 'creatives', it is the responsibility of us all.

While Schneider Electric, IBM and BLP all use video as a primary awareness medium, it's important to remember that these videos are just one element in a multi-channel, multi-platform, multi-format approach for their wider marketing activities. There are three lessons we can learn from them:

1 Creativity is a **competitive advantage**, providing differentiation and driving business value.
2 **Real stories from real people** create an emotional hook and capture attention in a way that features and benefits simply can't.
3 A **long-term brand 'platform'** creates wider impact: focus on one thing and do it well; a big idea, simply told, told over time, sticks in customers' hearts and minds.

This is our challenge as B2B marketers – to make the impossible possible, to inspire and defy the status quo, and to create a culture and environment where marketing can create magic. Even in 'boring' B2B.

What makes a great B2B marketer? 08

The majority of up and coming marketers today simply do not have the proper grounding in the marketing discipline; and they don't believe they need it. They firmly believe that marketing today is completely different from everything that came before, so the past does not apply. In B2B – and professional services in particular – we've done little to disprove or change this thinking. Too many of the people we hire or those who are already a part of our teams do not know or care about the history, the theory or the fundamental marketing principles and techniques that must be learned in order to become more than great project managers or tacticians. They simply don't possess the rigour, knowledge or wider thinking that is critical to understanding what drives and grows a business.

In previous chapters, I've already discussed why it's vitally important to get back to the marketing basics. In this chapter I explore what we need to do to identify and bring along the next generation of marketers, the qualities and background we need to be looking for, and the thinking we need to do on how we structure our teams and functions. I also explore the dilemma we face both with our marketing leadership and as leaders within B2B marketing.

Four essential qualities of great marketers

What really makes the difference between a good marketer and a great one? Solid technical marketing skills that we continually learn and hone throughout our careers combined with the marketing fundamentals are critical, but I've found that the best marketers also have these four essential underlying qualities:

1 **Curiosity**: Curiosity is probably the number one quality I look for when hiring. The best marketers are infinitely curious. They ask questions, lots of

questions, of both themselves and the business. They aren't afraid of what might be perceived as the 'stupid questions', because they really want to understand what's important and why. They want to know about you, your business, the market, the wider world. They have a real thirst for knowledge and understanding, and as a result a desire for and commitment to continuous improvement, to constantly renew and innovate their thinking, and to ultimately become better marketers.

2 **Thinking that goes beyond marketing:** In B2B marketing there are a lot of great project managers and specialist marketers. But I look for marketers who know how to think. That's why I tend towards a bias for those who have at least some experience outside of marketing or are educated beyond a marketing qualification. While a specific marketing background or marketing qualification clearly demonstrates a commitment to marketing as a profession, we as marketers need to think beyond what we do. For example: a literature degree highlights the building blocks of a great story and how underlying messages are communicated; a public policy background incorporates human perceptions, emotional triggers, and influencing; and a business degree lays the foundation for understanding what drives and grows a commercial enterprise.

   One of the best marketers I ever hired actually had a university degree in theatre studies, with a particular emphasis on stage design and management. At first glance, this type of qualification may not have much to do with marketing. But what this person brought to the team was an understanding and knowledge of the wider environment in which a story is told, and the elements that are necessary to enhance and embellish that story from an audience (read customer) perspective.

3 **Willingness to challenge:** The business environment in which we are working is unlike any that has come before. While marketing fundamentals may remain the same, the old measures of marketing 'success' are no longer relevant. The customer buying journey has fundamentally changed and we must change with it. This means doing things differently, in ways we may have never tried before. The best marketers challenge the status quo and are always looking to push the boundaries of what they and their organizations think marketing can and should do.

4 **Customer perspective:** There's a lot of talk about customer engagement and customer experience these days, and I've explored both in detail in previous chapters. But I've found that many marketers don't understand what this truly means; they are still too focused on what marketing does instead of

what is really of value to their business. So I look for marketers whose thinking begins and ends with the customer, who view all their marketing activity through the eyes of their customers and continually ask themselves: does this matter (to our customers)?

The seven behaviours of the most successful marketers

Last year I was on a flight back to London and the person sitting next to me was reading *The 7 Habits of Highly Effective People* by Dr Stephen Covey, who was considered a world-renowned authority on leadership. This little book was published in 1989 and has sold more than 20 million copies in over 40 languages worldwide, and remains one of the bestselling business books of all time.

Twenty-five years on, sitting on that plane, I remembered loving this book, yet I hadn't revisited it in a long time. I finally sat down to read it again and even though the language of the times has changed, I realized that Covey's seven habits could be interpreted as the behaviours of the best marketers I know.

Here are my seven behaviours of great marketers, adapted and reordered from Covey's 'Habits' (which are italicized in parentheses):

1 **Have a strategy** (*begin with the end in mind*): I've already discussed at length the need to begin with marketing strategy. We need to be very clear about what we are trying to achieve, our purpose and goals. If we don't understand where we want to get to, what we want to accomplish or who we want to engage with, we won't be able to develop plans and activities that are relevant, meaningful and measurable. We will end up just doing a lot of 'marketing stuff'.

2 **Take the time to plan and then execute brilliantly** (*put first things first*): Marketing, if done well, is fluid by nature. But we need to get better at planning, particularly at planning *flexibly*. We need to take the time to think through our plans and understand the steps we need to take in order to best achieve our strategic intent. Tactical expertise is not enough, but neither is strategy or planning. Because that strategy and those plans are worthless without the ability to execute to the highest standards. The best marketers not only do things right, they do the right things.

3 **Start by listening** (*seek first to understand, then to be understood*): Our customers don't want to be 'sold to' any more, so knowing our customers has never been more important. Marketing has traditionally been all about our business, what we have to offer, what we're selling, pushing out our messages to a passive audience through one-way channels. But marketing is no longer about what our businesses want to tell our customers, it's about listening to our customers and engaging in a way that offers meaning or value to them. What do our customers really care about? Do we engage with them about the things that really matter to them? Are we really listening to our customers or do we hear only what we want to hear?

4 **Engage** (*synergize*): Human beings have been creating, listening to and sharing stories since we first developed ways to communicate. Stories are how we connect, interact and collaborate as human beings. The best marketers are great at engaging people through the stories they tell, about themselves and the wider world, as well as about their organization's products and services.

5 **Take risks** (*be proactive*): While the fundamental principles of marketing have not changed, our customers have, and the ways in which we perform our jobs must change along with them. Taking risks and being proactive is also about taking responsibility for attempting what may never have been done before and being prepared to learn as well as fail. The best marketers challenge the status quo and are always looking to push the boundaries of what their organizations think marketing can do.

6 **Evaluate** (*think win–win*): Lately it seems like we are so caught up in demonstrating marketing ROI that I worry we are losing sight of whether we are actually achieving what we set out to do. Ultimately we want to engage and make an impact with our customers, creating differentiation, and becoming memorable in their hearts and minds. ROI as we know it does not adequately demonstrate this impact or differentiation. The best marketers don't just look at what can be measured, they evaluate for themselves, based on their marketing goals and objectives, what is and is not working for the business.

7 **Be curious and learn from everyone** (*sharpen the saw*): What are our competitors doing? What's the latest in the B2C world? What can we learn from companies like Coca-Cola and Cadbury's and Volvo? What are the best marketers doing to constantly renew and innovate their thinking? We need to make sure we take opportunities to engage with

other marketers, no matter whether they are B2B, B2C or agencies, so we can talk about the challenges we face, have conversations around new ideas, learn new things and be inspired.

Habits and behaviours are really interesting – they are what we do in life and work. They are learned, consciously and unconsciously. Behaviours are an amalgamation of our aspirations and our abilities – why we do what we do (what motivates us and the gifts or talents we have for attaining that aspiration) and how we do it (the foundation of experience and acquired knowledge that takes us in a certain direction).

For B2B marketers, one of the first steps that will enable us to be different is to become more conscious of our ingrained habits and behaviours and recognize our unconscious default activities.

How are we using our time?

A big part of Covey's book was about time management and it's relevant for everyone, no matter whether it's applied professionally or personally.

A large proportion of B2B marketers seem to be constantly busy, with never enough time to do everything that they need to do. For many of us, our days often feel like a constant fire-drill with barely enough time to breathe, much less think. We have lunch at our desks, and arrive early and stay late in the office. Yet how much of what we do during the day perhaps shouldn't even be done at all? We need to stop scurrying around like hamsters on a wheel and stop doing those things that do not contribute to what we must do as B2B marketers.

I would suggest we need to take a closer look at how we actually spend our time during an average day. I remember taking a Covey time management workshop many years ago, together with the rest of my team, although I actually don't remember anything at all about that workshop – not where or when I took it, the workshop facilitator, the other people there, not even who my boss was at the time. But I do remember a simple 2×2 matrix that I have adapted for B2B marketers (Figure 8.1).

This matrix represents the choices we make for utilizing our time during any given workday. Let's look at these quadrants more closely:

1 **Urgent/Important**: These are the tasks and activities we simply must complete each day or week. I don't ever really worry about these things because I know I'll always complete them. For B2B marketers, they tend to be things that are deadline driven, like media or production deadlines

Figure 8.1 Time management for B2B marketers

	Urgent	Not Urgent
Important	• Media and other deadlines • Completing project/campaign milestones such as writing briefs, proofing/approving copy, etc • Product launch activity	• Thinking time: strategy/planning/evaluation • Networking and learning: taking relevant courses or going to relevant events • Reading: B2B industry reports or marketing-related news, reports and articles
Not Important	• Reactive to interruptions and demands from the business • False deadlines: 'I need this now!' • Most phone calls, e-mails and meetings	• Busy work • Some social media • Chit-chat

SOURCE Adapted from Covey (1989)

and product launches, and all the day-to-day tasks necessary for ongoing good marketing management of programmes and campaigns. There are also some phone calls and e-mails that must be made, some meetings that must be attended and some social media activity that must be done as part of the 'day job'.

2 **Not Urgent/Important:** This is actually the most important quadrant in the matrix and the one we pay the least attention to. For all of us, no matter our level, it represents the crucial thinking or learning time that is critical for our specific B2B marketing role and longer-term goals. It's the bit that focuses not on what we do (the tasks), but how we do it (the strategy, planning, thinking, learning or ideas). Time spent in this quadrant is what ultimately turns good marketers into great marketers. Yet we get so caught up in the day-to-day doing of our jobs that far too little of our attention is spent in this quadrant. The activity that falls into this quadrant should be things like: developing and refining our marketing plans; paying attention to our professional development; and staying up to date with the reading related to our roles.

3 **Urgent/Not Important:** I'm constantly surprised at how much time we spend in this quadrant without even realizing it. Urgent tasks are what

keep us busy and they *feel* important even when they're not. We prioritize them in the moment and we derive a great sense of accomplishment from them. These are generally all the myriad interruptions that happen throughout the day – from the boss who needs a PowerPoint presentation done *this minute* to the stakeholder who needs a copy of the most recent publication *right now* to the event organizer who has such a great 'opportunity' to talk to us about. The vast majority of meetings also fall into this quadrant. If we can just become a little bit more aware of these things, we might be able to learn how to say 'No' a little more often to those things that don't provide value, for either ourselves or our organizations.

4 **Not Urgent/Not Important:** These are the time-wasters, the distractions, the things we do when we're tired and don't want to have to think too much, the things that always end up on the bottom of the to-do list but are easy to tick. How many things do we do on a daily basis that don't really need to be done at all? Do we go onto Twitter or LinkedIn for a real purpose, or just to see what we've missed? These are the things we need to eliminate as much as we can.

> Time is the scarcest resource and unless it is managed nothing else can be managed. (Peter Drucker, 1967)

If we can only ask ourselves these two questions – 'Is it urgent? Is it important?' – and incorporate this mental habit into our everyday working lives, we may find ourselves ultimately moving towards becoming better marketers with the time to become even better ones.

The qualifications debate

Last year, Mark Ritson wrote an article in *Marketing Week* that stirred up a firestorm among the marketing community. It was titled: 'Maybe it's just me, but shouldn't an expert in marketing be trained in marketing?' His premise was that, 'Before anyone is declared an expert/ninja/guru/visionary in marketing they need to learn the discipline. You need a qualification to be qualified.' His main point was that the new breed of marketing experts are big on tactics and light on marketing fundamentals, 'confined to a very small tactical box' which is really only a small part of the entire marketing discipline. And that these so-called experts are exerting an undue influence upon the next generation of marketing professionals.

What was so extraordinary wasn't even the article itself, it was the astonishing number of comments outraged by Mark's suggestion that marketers learn the discipline before they call themselves a marketing 'expert'. Beyond the outrage, the comments refuting Mark's point invariably used knowledge of a tactic (almost exclusively digital) as their example of their opposing point of view.

Which left me to wonder: *Does marketing have an inferiority complex?*

Are you qualified for B2B marketing?

We are what we do and we do what we know and learn. The reality is that a preponderance of marketers within the majority of our B2B organizations have no formal marketing training. Full stop. This is in direct contrast to the consumer marketing world, where B2C organizations actively look for marketers who have classical marketing training. Across B2B, there are an awful lot of marketers who haven't been schooled in what makes up the very foundations of marketing: brand, strategy, customer and market segmentation, positioning, and all the other essential thinking and actions that must happen before we ever actually start in on the tactical elements of what we do.

Because of this, I wonder if just maybe there is a niggling little suspicion in the back of our minds that we don't quite know what we're doing or why.

One of the biggest challenges we face as B2B marketers goes to the heart of the qualifications debate. There is a pervading perception within our organizations that marketing is not a 'proper' profession. And although this is really annoying, how else do we explain the lingering epitaphs of '*the colouring-in department*' and the '*party-planners*'? This perception is not helped by the tendency – especially in professional services organizations – to hire people who are great project managers or have the 'right' attitude, but have little else to recommend them as marketers.

> In what other profession is it the norm to have no qualifications?

Please don't get me wrong, I'm totally for anyone who wants to join this terrific profession of ours. Many things can and should be learned 'on the job', especially with today's rapidly changing technology environment and constant proliferation of new tools and channels. But when was the last time any of us were taught marketing fundamentals on the job? Never.

Ritson has a valid point; who is teaching the next generation of B2B marketers, what are we teaching them and how are we continuing their training throughout their careers? Furthermore, how are we continuing our own learning? These are important questions to ask of ourselves and our organizations. The giant consumer brands like P&G and Unilever have a clear career path for marketers within their organizations, alongside the relevant programmes and specific courses they need as they continue along that path. But I have not come across a single B2B brand that provides anything near the equivalent for their marketing teams.

Many marketers argue that a university marketing degree does not prepare anyone for the 'real world' of marketing. Frankly, I don't understand this argument; it could be made for every single profession in this day and age. Even an athlete – who could be claimed to learn by doing – has coaches, spends many hours learning the theory behind why they must perform in a certain way, attends lectures and seminars, and grounds themselves in the technical aspects of their sport in order to have the foundation upon which to improve and grow.

Marketing history, theory and principles have not changed. Marketing used to be taught solely as a supplemental module within a business degree, yet it's now taught at many universities throughout the world as a discipline in its own right. At undergraduate level, marketing degrees are available both as a BA (Bachelor of Arts) and a BSc (Bachelor of Science). The main difference between a Marketing BA and a Marketing BSc is that a BA involves more of an emphasis on the humanities, while a BSc focuses more on the scientific, mathematical and technological aspects of marketing. There are also professional marketing accreditations widely available from the likes of the Chartered Institute of Marketing (CIM), the Communication Advertising and Marketing Foundation (CAM), PRINCE2 and Google Analytics.

Granted, having a marketing qualification does not automatically equate to marketing excellence. But marketing does not exist in a vacuum; being exposed to and understanding the fundamentals of the wider business and undergoing training for the complete marketing discipline does create marketers who have a more holistic perspective of the business world and how marketing fits into that world.

Of course, we all know individuals and can point to people who have been hugely successful without any kind of formal qualifications. But I'm not talking about the outliers here – they are the exception and not the rule.

Tactical expertise is not enough. Great project management is not enough. If we want to be great marketers, not just good specialists, and to be taken seriously by our organizations, by those others within our organizations who do have a qualification, then a marketing qualification is a necessity. We must be marketers who fundamentally understand what drives and grows a business. We must be marketers who intimately know the landscape and commercials for our organizations, and whose thinking begins and ends with a deep understanding of the markets we operate in, our customers' buying behaviours and what motivates them.

This is the type of learning that is grounded in formal marketing training. Because what we learn there is the foundation for all marketing and it has not changed, no matter what the so-called experts are telling us.

Should marketers have an MBA?

Marketing is *not* just about what we do, it's about how we think and how we work across our organizations. The brilliant Peter Drucker said it best:

> Marketing... is not a specialized activity at all. It encompasses the entire business. It is the whole business seen from the point of view of the final result, that is, from the customer's point of view.

This is the catch; very few of us in B2B marketing actually look at marketing in the context of the wider business or even the wider commercial landscape in which we operate, much less from a truly customer perspective. This is particularly pertinent for B2B marketers because our marketing environment is so much more complex than in B2C. We are busy 'doing marketing' in the moment, instead of being marketers who are able to navigate this more complicated landscape and create the longer-term customer relationships necessary for the sustainability of our businesses. We don't know any better than what we 'do', because this is how most of us have been taught, this is how most of us have learned.

A Master's in Business Administration (MBA) is one of the most uniquely useful qualifications for anyone working in business. I firmly believe that if we had more marketers with MBAs, we'd have better marketers. Why?

Three reasons to get an MBA

1 A more holistic perspective and wider knowledge of the business world

I don't doubt that we're able to become technically proficient marketers without an MBA or other qualification.

But marketing is just one aspect of a business. Why wouldn't we want to better understand the world in which we're building our careers? Wouldn't we be better marketers if we had greater insight into how Finance, Operations, HR and all the other parts of a business actually worked? As well as what it all means within the global environment in which we're competing?

An MBA prepares us to think about business at a much higher level and to see the big picture. More importantly, it gives us the chance to learn and think about the issues that impact not only our business, but our customers, and on a much wider scale. This, in turn, provides us with the opportunity to better understand if and how 'what we do' matters.

2 New skills and knowledge

An MBA's core purpose is to prepare people for senior management and leadership roles. Chances are we will often need to work in teams in our current marketing roles, and as we progress in our careers we will eventually lead and manage teams. Practical leadership, teamworking and management skills are simply not taught 'on the job' in most of our organizations, but they are core to MBA programmes.

Furthermore, an MBA provides an interdisciplinary approach, drawing on fields as diverse as psychology, sociology, economics, accounting and finance. And, of course, marketing. The marketing module of an MBA covers the history, theory and fundamental principles that I've already discussed. Importantly, it does all this within the context of the entire organization. This is particularly significant in the B2B marketing environment because it helps us to better understand the issues and challenges our individual customers may be facing within their own organizations.

For example, how many of us ever consider the impact of macro- and micro-economics on 'what we do'? Where do we learn about individual or organizational buying behaviour and decision-making? Or how the wider economy might support or change those behaviours?

Beyond the standard business skills, however, an MBA focuses on the critical thinking and analytical skills that are lacking within the marketing profession. These skills are more important now than they have ever been for marketers and we rarely are able to learn these skills 'on the job'.

But we don't know what we don't know. And we don't know what the people we're learning from 'on the job' don't know. An MBA programme provides a structured environment in which to learn not only the marketing discipline itself but also the far-reaching elements that influence marketing.

3 Credibility

Having an MBA doesn't necessarily mean you'll be a better marketer.

Yet, rightly or wrongly, an MBA is a credential that sends a signal to the marketplace and to other people throughout our organizations. An MBA gives us the credibility that many marketers simply don't have, especially if we're in an industry where the people we work with outside of marketing are required to have a professional qualification.

For a profession that is struggling to be taken seriously at the highest levels of our organizations, an MBA better enables us to be seen as having an in-depth understanding of the entire business, as authorities in our own right and not 'just' as a support function. This then provides the foundation from which we can become more effective in 'what we do'.

Of course, an MBA isn't an option for a lot of people; it's expensive, time-consuming and really hard work. Yet there are a whole range of accredited MBA course options out there as well as a wide range of institutions and fees. Many of our organizations will sponsor further learning, including an MBA, in whole or in part. The time passes anyway. When I took my own MBA, there was a person in my year who – due to work, family, financial and other life commitments – had taken only one class per semester over nine years to achieve their diploma.

Whether or not for good reason, MBAs have come under fire over the past few years. The main argument against an MBA is similar to the argument against all marketing qualifications – that the institutions providing the qualification have become stagnant and aren't responding fast enough to the rapidly changing and increasingly dynamic business world. There are those who believe the curricula are outdated and simply no longer relevant.

While we all know that the business world has changed, just like the marketing fundamentals many things remain timeless. Studying for an MBA provides the environment for experimentation, problem-solving, and the testing of new thinking. But most importantly, it can give us the commercial grounding, wider business foundation and insight into our customers' businesses that just may offer us what we need to make it to the B2B C-suite.

I absolutely believe that every marketer – especially those who want to be leaders – should have an MBA, even though this often isn't realistic for our profession. I look more closely at leadership in the next chapter, but what other options are there for continued learning and growth within our profession?

What conference?

A career in marketing has always meant constant reinvention. When I started out, there were a mere handful of tactics and channels that made up a B2B marketer's 'toolkit' – PR, events, direct mail and our product datasheets were pretty much it. I could never have predicted the dramatic changes that were in store for me, the companies I worked for, or our customers.

One of the biggest mistakes we make as B2B marketers is that too often we get stuck in our silos, in our organizations, and don't venture out into the wider world of our profession. We simply don't look beyond what we do or know and we tend to rely on the marketing activity that has always worked for us.

But we need to stop doing what we have always done and start asking ourselves: are we really doing the right things? We must continue to learn and grow within our profession. This doesn't mean just learning about new technology, or the latest tools, tactics and channels. What are our competitors doing? What's the latest in the B2C world? What are the best marketers doing to constantly renew and update their thinking?

There are thousands of marketing conferences held throughout the year across the globe. There are specialist conferences, generalist conferences, regional conferences and global conferences on every conceivable marketing topic, tactic, channel and platform. Three of these are a must-attend for me every year in the UK – Marketing Week Live (MWL – held in March), B2B Ignite (formerly the B2B Marketing Summit – held in June) and the Festival of Marketing (FoM – held in October). MWL and FoM are primarily B2C focused but have B2B streams; and as I've emphasized before, B2B can learn a lot from the B2C marketing world. Michael Brenner's annual 'Ultimate guide to the best marketing conferences', published every January, is a terrific source for conferences around the world.

It is difficult to decide which one or combination of all the conferences out there might be best for our particular needs, given our level and skills. Read the agendas, find out more about the speakers, and just go to one. These marketing conferences are vitally important. We need to make sure we take these opportunities to engage with other marketers, no matter whether they are B2B, B2C or agencies. We simply must talk about the challenges we face, listen to how others are solving those challenges, have conversations around new ideas, learn new things and be inspired.

I didn't always feel this way; I thought going to a marketing conference would be a complete waste of my time. I made all kinds of excuses – I'm far too busy, I can't take an entire day out of the office, it won't add value to my day-to-day job, on and on.

Then about five or six years ago, I attended my first B2B marketing event. It was at a time when the commercial landscape for my business was undergoing a radical transformation and I was completely changing my approach to marketing, developing a very different marketing strategy within my organization. If you'll recall, five or six years ago we were still in the early days of 'digital' within B2B and 'social media' was barely a whisper in the B2B marketing world. And I was getting an awful lot of push-back around my approach from within my company.

That B2B conference was a 'Eureka!' moment for me and became a complete validation of what I was doing. For the first time, I heard from and spoke to marketers who were moving in the same direction I was, struggling to get to grips with technology we didn't yet completely understand, and not quite certain what it meant for our businesses. I left that event with renewed confidence; it was like a light bulb went off in my head, and not only have I continued to attend marketing conferences ever since, I have ensured that my teams do so as well.

It is not always easy to get ourselves and our people out to these conferences. We're incredibly busy, all the time, our Learning and Development (L&D) budgets have been squeezed into near non-existence and too often our leadership doesn't understand the value of this type of day out of the office.

We must make the time and find a way.

Five reasons for attending at least one marketing conference this year

1. **Best-practice marketing**: While marketing fundamentals remain the same, the old ways of working and the old measures of marketing 'success' are no longer relevant. The pace of change gets faster and faster; with the right agenda and speakers, a marketing conference is an intensive learning experience from the very best marketers about what's working and what's not.
2. **Next-practice marketing**: It's not just insight into best practice that's important for marketers. What's on the horizon that we need to start thinking about now? At the best conferences we have a chance to hear from the top thinkers as well as practitioners in our profession, across many different companies and industries.

3 **Challenge our thinking**: Not everything we see and hear may be relevant, and, unfortunately, many of the so-called 'experts' out there simply aren't. But it's essential to constantly challenge how we think and what we do as marketers. And it's just as important to learn to recognize the good from the bad and downright awful.

4 **Online doesn't have all the answers**: Despite the omnipresence of our digital world, nothing takes the place of face-to-face. There is just so much 'stuff' out there, even for us marketers! Sure, there's a wealth of information on just about everything we could conceivably want to know. But there's also a lot that's just plain bad advice or incorrect information, and it's often hard to know the difference. Face-to-face also gives us the opportunity to ask questions, hear answers to questions asked by others we may have never even thought of, and participate in debate with a widely diverse group of people.

5 **Networking**: Like the old BT advert, 'It's good to talk.' Many of us are terrific networkers within our own organizations; but too often, particularly when our markets and our businesses are in the midst of change, this internal networking merely validates what we've always done, instead of exploring what we need to do differently. Attending a conference exposes us to all sorts of people we might not otherwise meet, across all sorts of industries, giving us a diversity of opinions and perspectives that we may not have within our own organizations.

Network, network, network

Networking is a skill, one of the most important we can learn as marketers. Just like our technical marketing skills, networking is a skill that needs to be learned and it must be continually practised to be improved.

In the previous section I touched on networking as a key benefit for attending a marketing conference. But there are all kinds of networking activities out there. For example, here in the UK we have a dedicated community of B2B marketers, agencies and consultants called the Business Marketing Club (BMC), which provides a monthly forum for B2B marketers to meet up, discuss our challenges and exchange ideas.

Yet networking is also hard work. I attended a small conference recently where one of the speakers spoke about some of the behavioural and cultural characteristics of great leaders. At one point in the presentation, the speaker asked the roomful of senior B2B marketers to rank themselves on two questions:

- How often do you network?
- How good do you feel you are at networking?

Surprisingly (or perhaps not), the vast majority of people in the room ranked themselves poor at both. When asked why, the overwhelming sentiment was that networking is a chore, it's time-consuming and tiring, and doesn't really have anything to do with a marketer's 'day job'.

I can understand that. For years, a very savvy (and extremely well networked) mentor of mine encouraged me ad nauseam to get involved in networking outside of my company. Like the marketers at that event, I made the same excuses.

I simply cannot emphasize enough the importance of networking – no matter where we are or what we may do in our careers. Most of us learn to be great internal networkers, within our own companies; it is, after all, how we gain sponsorship for our marketing activity, navigate internal politics and create a path for advancement.

Eight critical reasons to network outside of our own organizations

1. **Build relationships** across a wide spectrum of industries and organizations, both horizontally and vertically.
2. **Find sponsors and mentors** who can give us new and different perspectives.
3. **Engage with peers** and hear what other marketers are doing in different organizations.
4. Break out of our organizational mindset, **learn new things** and be inspired.
5. Gain **ongoing support** throughout our careers.
6. Develop **a sounding board** for our ideas and **a reality check** for our plans.
7. Discover new paths to **that next big step** in our careers.
8. Create a pool for **spotting talent** for our own organizations that we might never come across.

A career in marketing? Advice to my younger self

My career as a B2B marketer has now spanned more than two decades; I've worked for five different organizations over that time, across multiple industries and continents. And while a lot has changed over the years, a lot has also remained the same. A few years ago, LinkedIn hosted a series of posts where they invited professionals to share the advice that they might give to their younger selves. That series inspired me to think about what I know now that I wished I'd known then. What advice would I give to my younger self just starting a career in marketing? These are just five things I wish I had understood better when I was starting out:

- **The job description really does not describe the job**: too often it's an aspiration rather than a reality. Unfortunately, in B2B marketing, those doing the hiring and thus writing the job description may 'talk the talk' but are still stuck in the outdated ways of thinking, doing and being. This happens for every generation entering the working world, not just marketing. So, be prepared to create and recreate your role. We all bring our own unique personalities, skills, knowledge and perspectives to whatever job we take on, so the job ultimately becomes what we make of it.
- **Ask a lot of questions, even the seemingly 'stupid' ones**: the ability to ask the right questions is critical to marketing success. The best marketers are infinitely curious – because they really want to understand what's important and why, to the business and to customers. The great Peter Drucker once said that, 'The only thing we know about the future is that it will be different.' Having a real thirst for knowledge and discovery is what ultimately creates better marketers.
- **Your company does not love you**: do not misplace your loyalty. Your company will *always* do what's best for the company and this doesn't always translate to what is best for *you*. While you absolutely must work to the best of your capabilities for your employer, you also have a responsibility to yourself. So, don't just think about the job you're doing now, think about the job you want to have next, and the one you want after that. Think about where you want to go and what you want to happen in your career, and make sure you are getting what you need to take those next steps.

- **Go on secondment to another country**: and while you're at it, be sure to learn the language. Living and working in another country will stretch you in ways you never dreamed of. Another place, another culture and another language will compel you to look at yourself and what you do in completely different ways. You will experience different working practices and organizational structures; it will test your flexibility and adaptability as an employee; and even open up other opportunities. It's also a fantastic way to see other parts of the world.
- **Never stop learning**: marketing is all about continuous learning, learning is about discovery and 'discovery consists of seeing what everybody has seen and thinking what nobody has thought' (Albert Szent-Györgyi, Nobel Prize in Medicine, 1937). So attend marketing conferences, hear what other professionals are thinking and doing; take a class to improve a skill; go for an MBA if you can and if you can't, then be a voracious reader of the news, business and industry journals, and fiction.

The leadership dilemma in B2B marketing 09

What makes a great leader? Clearly, there's no easy answer to this question; I found 178,051 books on the subject on Amazon in English alone. On Google I found 792 million results in answer to my query, including pages and pages and pages of blogs, courses, training and articles on the '7 traits, 10 qualities, 5 skills, 16 characteristics' of great leaders, and more.

One of the best definitions of a leader I've found comes from an article by online resource Mindtools, who deliver leadership, team and personal development training to individuals, businesses, government agencies and nonprofits worldwide. Mindtools defines leaders as people who 'help themselves and others to do the right things. They set direction, build an inspiring vision, and create something new' (Mindtools, 2017).

This is an important distinction. As Peter Drucker said, 'Management is doing things right; leadership is doing the right things.' Thus, leadership is a responsibility, and it is hard work.

There is an interesting paradox to leadership. Ultimately, followers will only ever be perceived in the manner in which their leadership is perceived and a leader will only ever be as effective as their followers.

Should marketing have a seat on the board in B2B?

Inevitably, no matter the organization, marketing will only ever be as good as the marketing leadership. Having a seat in the boardroom as chief marketing officer (CMO) is considered the pinnacle of marketing leadership. There are far fewer CMOs in B2B than there are in B2C and this has been the topic of much discussion and debate in B2B marketing forums in recent years.

Yet I'm concerned that having a focus on the boardroom overshadows and sidesteps many of the questions that we should be asking of our marketing leadership. We are facing far bigger, more immediate challenges within our B2B marketing functions which need to be addressed before we even think about our representation on the board. Chief among these is that marketing in B2B continues to be perceived as fulfilling an 'order-taker' or support role, which is not really valued by the business.

I therefore consider discussions about marketing having a seat on the board as really being about the value and influence that marketing brings to the business.

Many marketers tell me the issue is that they need to get better at speaking 'the language of the business' in order to demonstrate that value and achieve that influence. I would actually go further than that – I would suggest that there is a fundamental lack of understanding of what actually drives and grows a business. If we want to sit on the board, we absolutely must have an understanding of our business and its markets beyond marketing.

This is an important point: B2B marketers will not have a seat at the top table if they do not come out of their marketing silos to understand and tackle the wider business issues, many of which marketing is uniquely positioned to address. The marketers who understand this, contributing to the achievement of those wider business goals, will be the ones who ultimately take their rightful place in the boardroom.

Why should anyone be led by you?

Leadership doesn't just exist in corporate boardrooms, of course, it exists throughout society, in many spheres and at all levels. One of the best books I've ever read on leadership was *Why Should Anyone Be Led by You?* by Rob Goffee and Gareth Jones (2006). The book is dedicated to 'all those who strive to lead organizations' but it's a very interesting read for anyone who aspires to any type of leadership or currently leads a team, a function or even a single project. It's also highly relevant for B2B marketers, many of whom are positioning their organizations as market leaders, their people as thought leaders or themselves as marketing leaders within their organizations.

The subtitle of the book is *What it takes to be an authentic leader* and its main premise is that great leaders are 'authentic' leaders. They know who they are, where their organizations need to go, and how to take their followers along with them.

The many entertaining and real examples of leadership in practice throughout the book underscore that there is no formula for leadership. Yet the authors' position around authenticity really resonated with me. Because just like our customers – who want to buy from people and organizations that they like to do business with, whose values align with their own, with whom they can build long-term relationships and with whom they can really feel connected on an emotional level – we want leaders we feel are worth following.

This sounds obvious, that a great leader is someone we want to follow. But I often see those who are aspiring to leadership – or are in fact leaders of a function, team or project – focus on managing people or the function itself instead of being leaders. Or they do what they think leaders do, not what their followers or their business actually want or need from them.

In a world where our customers are now looking for authenticity in the organizations they do business with, marketing has a real opportunity to provide leadership for our B2B businesses by helping them move from 'selling' to 'engagement'. This is another battleground for marketing and where we can deliver that value for which we crave recognition: to engage with our customers in meaningful and inspiring ways that create long-term relationships and turn those relationships into customers for our businesses.

For me, this is what leadership is really all about: the ability to engage, inspire and communicate in compelling and authentic ways that make a leader worth following.

Five requirements for great marketing leadership

> To be a leader you must act like one, think like one, and speak like one, while remaining true to who you are. (Yetunde Hofmann, 2017)

Yetunde Hofmann is a leadership and change consultant whom I had the great privilege of hearing speak at a marketing conference about the cultural and behavioural requirements that make for great leadership.

What do our businesses expect from marketing, and, importantly, what do we want and expect from our marketing leadership? What does great leadership look like and how do we grow our leadership capability?

Yetunde spoke about five requirements that executive boards look for in a leader, and they are just as relevant for what we need to look for in our B2B marketing leadership:

1 **Vision**: Leaders have the ability to paint a picture of the future, tell a story about it, and move their people and organizations towards it.

2 **Strategic direction**: to achieve their vision, leaders have a deep understanding of the business landscape – competitive and economic, the trends that are influencing that landscape, and they develop a strategy that provides a clear direction for everyone in the business.
3 **Performance management**: Vision and strategy are meaningless without a solid awareness of what it takes to deliver that strategy, and leaders continually enable, empower and champion their people to do just that.
4 **Capability development**: Leaders focus not only on themselves, but on their people, making sure they have the necessary tools and technical capability. But more importantly, they also focus on developing other leaders at all levels throughout the organization.
5 **Stakeholder engagement**: Leaders are adept at dealing with and engaging both the internal organization and the external world, and bringing these people along with them.

These five dynamics lie at the heart of great leadership. Taken together, they are not about what leaders do and say, but how they behave – and it's how our leaders behave that makes them worth following.

Three 'A's for marketing leaders – authenticity, agility and affinity

More than ever before, we need leadership for our marketing functions and teams that challenges and inspires us to do, think and be different. There are three other attributes that we need to look for and cultivate in our people on their path towards leadership:

1 **Authenticity** is one of those words that's been used so much it's become almost meaningless. I often read that great leaders are authentic leaders, but what does that really mean? So I looked up the definition in the dictionary, where authenticity is defined as 'the quality of being authentic – real and genuine'.

But I like Yetunde's definition better:

> Authenticity is being yourself, with skill.

What this means to me is that great leaders are deeply self-aware; they know and understand who they are. The 'skill' part is in leading in a way that best reflects this 'self' and then elevating and imparting that 'self' in an engaging and appropriate way. Yetunde calls this 'being, on purpose'.

2. **Agility** is about responding to our increasingly complex, always-on world. Once again, I looked up the definition in my dictionary: agility is 'the ability to move, think and understand quickly and easily'.

   Our business environment is growing ever faster-paced and more dynamic. And most of our B2B organizations are in the midst of major transformation. This means that our marketing leaders must possess the ability to drive this change – not just react to it – by anticipating future trends, engaging stakeholders within the organization, aligning the organization behind the change and, most importantly, executing that change quickly and transparently.

3. **Affinity** is about building relationships and communicating. Once again, I looked up the definition in my dictionary: affinity is 'a natural liking for and understanding of someone... a relationship'.

   Great leaders are great networkers; they are intensely interested in people and are adept at building wide and diverse networks, both business and social. By continually engaging in a dialogue and an exchange of ideas with others, they are able to broaden their thinking, find new ideas, understand different perspectives, spot talent, and here I quote Yetunde again:

> Build relationships before they're needed.

I worry that our B2B marketing leaders do more of managing a function for the business and less of truly leading their people. As marketers, we crave leaders who challenge and inspire us to *think different*, *do different* and *be different*. An authentic, agile leader with affinity is a leader truly worth following.

Leaders create 'next practice', not just 'best practice'

I also had the great privilege of listening to a presentation by Nick Udall – CEO of a company called 'nowhere' and author of *Riding the Creative Rollercoaster* (2014) – who shared his passion and vision for the future of leadership. Nick works with CEOs who are recognizing that they are reaching a ceiling of capability in a world that is becoming more and more volatile, uncertain, complex and ambiguous – and is working with them in some truly unique ways.

Nick's main premise is that CEOs get to where they are by being good at what they do and because of what they know. But they can no longer rely on what they've always done in order to achieve sustainable and ongoing success for their organizations. Does this sound familiar? It should, because B2B marketers are facing the same dilemma. It's the *unknown* that is determining the future and it's the way our leaders take our people and organizations towards that unknown that creates real breakthroughs for businesses and real magic for marketers.

Key takeaways for B2B marketers:

- *Innovation* and *creativity* are the strategic differentiators for businesses. I've already discussed the dearth of creativity in B2B marketing and I really loved Nick's definitions of both innovation and creativity – innovation is 'bringing new to the world' and creativity is 'bringing the new to mind'.
- Successful organizations have a strong sense of *identity* and a clear sense of *purpose.*
- They create 'next practice' not just 'best practice'.
- *Next-generation leadership* is about unlocking the creativity of teams, communities and stakeholders.

I particularly liked Nick's description of *Innovation* as 'a co-creative dance between the known and the unknown'. This made me think of the line from a W B Yeats poem:

How can we know the dancer from the dance?

True leaders *become* the choreographers of this dance towards the future by continually pushing the boundaries between the known and unknown, and making their people and organizations a part of that dance.

Nick also said one other thing that made an impression on me: *Leaders are time-rich.* I took this to mean that leaders create time and space for themselves. This is quite thought-provoking given how busy so many B2B marketers appear to be, and reinforces the notion that our time is our own responsibility.

We have such an opportunity to provide leadership for our teams and our organizations by helping our people on this journey into and through ambiguity and uncertainty. We have a role to play in the evolution of our corporate culture and the potential to shape our markets. The central question is how fast marketing can learn what's wanted and needed, and how we can share that learning throughout our organizations. We can start by thinking bigger and more strategically, and acting more collaboratively outside of our marketing silos.

What do our CEOs want from marketing?

Business alignment, innovation, collaboration, market and customer intelligence, and creativity. In 2014, at the B2B Marketing Leaders Forum in London, Tom Stein presented Great Expectations – the results of his company's wide-ranging research into B2B CEOs to understand their perspectives on what CEOs care about and what their marketing leadership is delivering.

The research found that overall only 23 per cent of CEOs were extremely satisfied with their marketing leadership and that they had big unmet expectations of marketing in three key areas:

- Above all, CEOs wanted marketing to be innovators, creating differentiation for their brand and delivering on the brand promise.
- They wanted better alignment between marketing, sales and IT, and with the overall business strategy – with marketing thinking and acting more strategically outside of their marketing discipline.
- They were also looking to drive intimacy with their customers – and expected marketing to deliver ongoing customer engagement and customer insight.

This should have been a wake-up call for B2B marketing leaders, that such a disconnect existed between what's most important to CEOs and what marketing was delivering.

Yet at the end of 2016, according to a report from the CMO Council and Deloitte, while two-thirds of marketing leaders claimed that they wanted to focus on business strategy and innovate new approaches, the reality was that they were spending the bulk of their time reviewing marketing plans and budgets and attending meetings. The findings suggest that not much has changed since the 2014 Stein IAS report; marketing leaders and their teams are still struggling to step out of their marketing silos. The conclusion of the report was that if marketing is to have 'a greater role and impact, they will need to do a better job at demonstrating their business value and impact'.

The leadership dilemma remains. B2B marketing has not moved much closer to achieving our greater aspirations. Marketers remain 'doing' marketing and our marketing leadership remains stuck in the management aspects of their roles.

What makes a B2B marketing leader?

Our technical marketing skills will only get us so far. For many of us, that's fine; we'll certainly never get bored and if we keep on learning the new skills that new technology will invariably require, those skills will always be in demand. But if that's all we want, then we have got to stop complaining about marketing not having a seat on the board or that our business doesn't value us as much as we think it should.

If we want more – and different – then we need to ask ourselves some tough questions:

- Do we think as well as do?
- Do we create the new or maintain the status quo?
- Are we managers or leaders?
- Are we doing marketing, managing the doing of marketing, or are we leading marketing within our companies?
- Do we really know what our CEOs and the wider business want and need from us?
- What do we need to do to become marketing leaders and, further, to cultivate leadership throughout our marketing function?

This is the predicament we face, because most of us weren't born leaders. Most of us are great tacticians with the necessary technical skills to implement those tactics. Some of us are inevitably promoted to leadership positions because of those technical skills and our ability to get things done. But few of us have the necessary skills for leadership.

I mentor a very talented young marketer who has been on the 'fast track' within their marketing organization. Creative, technically adept, and with the ability to think and act far beyond their marketing silo, they had managed many projects and even some junior members of the team. When the leader of their team left the company, they applied for this much more senior role. Following a rigorous interview process, with other internal and external candidates, they were promoted to lead the team within which they had been such a success.

This extraordinarily capable marketer is struggling. They're struggling not because they aren't very good at what they do, they're struggling because they – and those who hired for the role – didn't understand that leading a team required a very different skill set from what had made them such a success in the first place.

We don't know what we don't know. This person continues to struggle because they aren't being given the training, the tools or the support to transform from a marketing manager into a marketing leader.

Becoming B2B marketing leaders

The first step to becoming a B2B marketing leader is to realize that what makes a great marketer doesn't necessarily translate into successful leadership. Just like the struggling young leader I mentor, if our organizations are not giving us the tools we need for being or becoming leaders, we must reach out to find this for ourselves. The next step is to stop the blame game. We are responsible for who we are and what we do. If our business does not value marketing, that is our fault, not the fault of the rest of the business. We have got to stop talking about 'educating' the business about marketing and start being more than 'just marketers'.

We must be different and redefine marketing in terms of the business. This is not about the language we use – although that's part of it – and it's not about the marketing outputs; it's fundamentally about the outcomes that are required by the business. If our outputs are not valued by the business, then we need to start doing what the business does value. We simply must get a whole lot better at listening to our businesses and understanding what they really want and need from us, instead of insisting that they value our technical skills.

In *The 12 Powers of a Marketing Leader* (2017), co-authors Thomas Barta and Patrick Barwise discuss their original research into the business impact and career success of senior marketers. In the research, they found 12 sets of leadership attributes, falling into four distinct categories, that determine marketing success. However, the book isn't about marketing, it's a book about leadership for marketers, and it's a profoundly important book for those of us in B2B marketing who are already leaders or who aspire to leadership.

Through their research, the authors unequivocally found that successful marketers weren't successful because of their technical marketing skills, their knowledge of the industry or their companies' products and services, or even because of their personalities – although these all did contribute in some measure to their success. Instead, they found that the primary driver of success for marketers was their leadership skills, with more than half citing these leadership skills as critical for marketing's ability to create a meaningful impact on their business and further their own careers.

The book is aligned around a simple premise: that marketing is uniquely positioned to be the voice of the customer within the company and drive alignment in what the authors call the 'Value Creation Zone (V-Zone)'. This is 'the space where customer needs and company needs overlap' and it's only through mastering and applying leadership skills that this V-Zone can be maximized.

The book takes us through the stages of learning these leadership skills, which the authors call the '12 Powers' – these involve mobilizing our bosses (shaping and influencing the agenda), our colleagues (for a more holistic customer approach) and our teams (becoming a leader of leaders). But most importantly, it involves mobilizing ourselves (finding purpose and inspiring others).

We all know that most of our B2B organizations are slow to change. Organizational behaviour and perceptions are deeply rooted, even within the fast-moving technology sector. It's up to each of us to take charge and make change happen, and the first step is to embody that change ourselves. It may feel daunting, risky and scary, but no matter where we sit in our organizations, we can make a start. Because we are marketers, we are people with a passion for our customers and our brands, and we can inspire change by learning the skills we need to become marketing leaders instead of people who just 'do' marketing.

Leading and structuring our teams

A large part of the responsibility of being a marketing leader is creating the right environment in which marketing can excel. This includes the overall marketing structure within the organization, the teams within that structure, and where marketing physically sits within the building that houses the business.

There is no one 'right' structure for a marketing function or team, but I've found that the most successful ones are aligned with how the business goes to market.

I know one marketing director who was brought in by a new business leader to head up the marketing team following a merger of two large companies. They inherited long-standing teams who delivered sales support that was reactive and ad hoc, operating in silos with mini-campaigns that were primarily events based. Their vision and subsequent marketing strategy resulted in the creation of a demand generation model that was top-down, driven by a hierarchy of integrated, end-to-end programmes for the core markets, with a centralized team for core processes and flagship research. Marketers were then aligned with the priority industries and propositions, focusing on thought leadership and lead generation activities to consistently engage with customers, with a dual objective of increasing both mindshare and market share for the brand. The overriding principle for the marketing team was to do fewer things but to commit to some big ideas for greater impact. In this way, they were able to create a simple marketing platform that could be scaled and adapted for specific parts of the business.

Similarly, another B2B marketing director inherited a small team in a much smaller company, but with many of the same challenges. The team were highly skilled technically, but were completely reactive to the demands of the salespeople; this marketing director quickly discovered that the business didn't really know what marketing did. They therefore first spent a lot of time meeting with the sales teams and other people throughout the organization to understand their priorities and how they went to market, and then put in place a structure that aligned with the company's go-to-market strategy, with marketers sitting alongside the business areas. With this structure in place, sales and marketing had day-to-day interactions with each other, there were some marketing 'quick wins' that the business didn't expect, and the business began to understand what marketing could do.

There's one very important lesson we can learn from both these examples. It doesn't necessarily matter what the team structure looks like as long as there are two key elements:

- The marketing structure is aligned with the business; in other words, how the business goes to market.
- No matter the structure, both the marketing team and the business must have clarity on what marketing does and does not do.

There's a third critical element that's aligned with these two points: Where do we physically sit within the business? Do we interact with our stakeholders on a daily basis? Do we see our salespeople going to or returning from meetings? Do we have the opportunities for those hallway chats that often provide us with valuable information about what's happening in our business and our markets, and with our customers? Do we actually talk to anyone outside marketing?

Dave Stevens, a CMO with over 20 years of B2B marketing experience across the public, private and voluntary sectors, told me the following story about his first day as UK marketing director for a very large global B2B organization:

> It's a beautiful summer's day and it's my first day as marketing director for this incredible company. My first meeting is on the eighth floor of the company's prestigious headquarters with the chairman and managing director (MD). There's a glorious view across the city. We talk about some of my ideas and my overall vision for the marketing function. The MD asks me to present to the company's leadership team the following month. Great, I'm on the agenda, the meeting has gone well and I'm excited to meet the marketing team, my second meeting of my first day on the job, where I will introduce myself to the team, talk about my vision, hopefully inspire, and start to get to know everyone.
>
> I leave the MD's office. I walk past the offices of the COO and CFO, past the desks of the heads of the different product and service lines, past the desks of the Internal Communications team, past the desks where the Business Development team sits. I pass the coffee vending machines and informal meeting area. I walk past the toilets. I walk out through a set of double doors, into the lift, down one floor, down another floor, and another. And another. And another. And one more. And then finally to the ground floor. I walk past the company restaurant, across the lobby, through the security barriers, across the large and impressive reception area. And then I walk outside of the building. Past a coffee shop. Past a sandwich shop. Past a grocery food retailer. Down a lane. Into another building, past a security desk, up two flights of stairs and onto the floor where there is a large and mostly empty hot desk area. I finally arrive at where the Marketing Department sits.

Dave's experience is not an isolated one. In many of our organizations, especially the larger ones, marketing physically sits in locations that are far removed from the day-to-day business. It's no wonder so many of us find it difficult to get out of our marketing silos.

There is a lot of ongoing debate about the structure of marketing teams and functions. In one of my previous companies, we had a significant marketing restructure every three to four years, coinciding with a complete change in our marketing leadership team. This happens all too often in an awful lot of our companies and only serves to underscore the fact that our business leaders are not happy with what marketing is delivering.

This is not a good kind of disruption; it creates ongoing uncertainty and confusion, which leads to a loss of productivity, not to mention low morale and job dissatisfaction. Yet for many of us in B2B, the continual restructuring of marketing has become the norm. We've been structured by industry, by product line and by capability; we've been centralized, decentralized and outsourced. In the process, we've lost more knowledge, capability and talent than we've gained, and instead of streamlining the marketing function or making it more effective, it's served only to perpetuate the mediocrity which remains inherent in the majority of marketing functions. We merely replace one ineffective structure with another.

Yet the structure is rarely the issue.

How we lead – providing clarity

Whether we are marketing leaders within large or small organizations, or we are leaders of teams or projects, one of the most important characteristics of leadership is to provide clarity – clarity of vision, clarity of purpose, clarity of plan and clarity of responsibility. The marketing teams that are most effective know where they are going, why they are going there, how they're going to do it and who is responsible. They are focused, inspired, committed, collaborative and productive. They don't waste time and they don't complain or blame. They just get on with it and deliver the value we all crave.

Twice a year, Sarah – a marketing director at a medium-sized software company – takes her team of twelve people on an away day, often with two or three specifically invited sales or operations people with whom they work closely. They hire a separate meeting venue outside of and completely away from the office, and no matter what is going on, they turn off their phones for the entire day. This day is in two parts – the first half is spent discussing strategy and plans – what's been working, what hasn't and what would work better if something were changed. They talk about what's happening in their markets, new ideas and new ways of doing what they do, and decide as a team where they will place their priorities. Everyone participates equally – from the most junior to most senior members of the team – and there are no slide presentations. Everyone leaves this part of the away day with something they personally commit to doing that they've not done before. The second half of the day is spent doing something fun – for example, to name just a few of the activities, they've been ten-pin bowling and ice-skating, they've had tea at the Savoy, they've done a room escape, and they've gone to a pub and had their own pub quiz, complete with prizes for the winning team.

These away days are all about achieving ongoing clarity and have been a critical part of the team's continuing success. It's a chance to evaluate, review and regroup, a time to think, share, celebrate achievements and build continuing trust in each other and what they do, as individuals and as a team. Sarah always receives feedback that these away days are inspiring and energizing.

Contrast this leadership approach with one for another team, this one an industry team within a very large corporate enterprise. Their annual away day is held within a large conference room at corporate headquarters and consists of each sub-sector leader giving a slide presentation on the marketing activity they've done over the past year and what they're planning for the coming year. This is followed by the industry marketing leader giving an update on the most recent marketing leadership meeting and the overall company financials.

Once they had a presentation from someone external to the company and once they had a presentation from the corporation's board member who has marketing oversight. Most of the members of this team dread these annual meetings and by the end of the day there is a palpable lack of energy or interest throughout the room. Drinks and nibbles are brought in at the end of the day, but most people quickly make their excuses and leave.

Which team would you rather be a part of?
Which type of leader would you prefer to be?

Objective-setting – creating the next generation of marketing leaders

In his 1954 book *The Practice of Management*, Peter Drucker introduced his concept of Management by Objectives (MBO), the essence of which is that individual objectives are developed in alignment with corporate objectives:

- Objectives are determined with employees.
- Objectives are formulated at quantitative and qualitative levels.
- Objectives are challenging and motivating.
- There is daily feedback or coaching instead of static management reports.
- Rewards (recognition, appreciation and/or performance-related pay) for achieving the intended objectives are a requirement.
- The basic principle is growth and development.

Out of this MBO concept has grown the SMART technique for setting objectives – Specific, Measurable, Achievable (sometimes Attainable), Realistic (sometimes Relevant) and Time-bound – which is pervasive and which the majority of us, including myself, have used for objective-setting throughout our careers (Figure 9.1). These are the objectives against which we receive feedback and are measured during our performance reviews, which are generally reflected in our pay packets. Setting objectives has generally been accepted as one of the responsibilities of management and we have accepted SMART as the way it ought to be done.

Yet, as I was exploring the role of leadership, I read an article that made me think about objective-setting in a totally new way.

Dick Grote – a performance management consultant with an early career spent at GE, United Airlines and Frito-Lay – argues in an article titled '3 popular goal-setting techniques managers should avoid' (2017) that SMART objectives may, in fact, be leading people to set low goals. In particular, he cites the work of two of the best-known academic researchers on goal-setting – professors Edwin A Locke and Gary P Latham – who found over the course of 35 years of research that specific, difficult goals with tight deadlines (irrespective of whether the goal is jointly set by the individual and manager, or whether the manager defines what's expected with a tough due-date) resulted in greater effort and better performance. Grote believes that while the SMART technique is useful, we need tough, demanding goals and objectives that really stretch us in order to achieve the highest levels of effort and performance.

Figure 9.1 SMART objectives

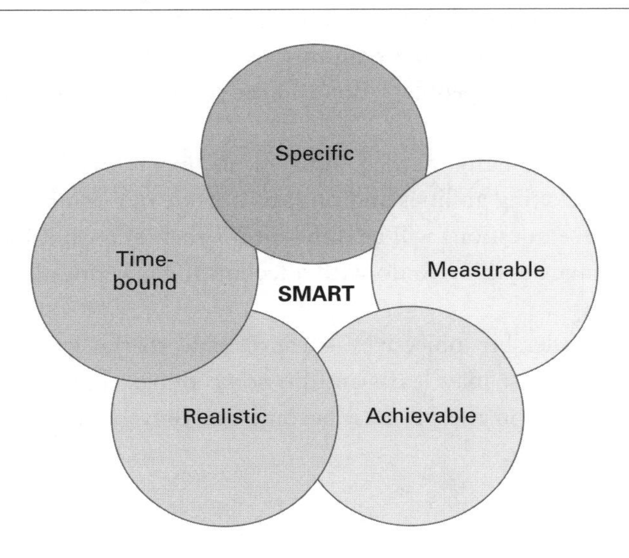

This article was an eye-opener for me, and reinforced how we seldom question 'what we've always done'. When I was in the corporate world, our annual goal-setting exercises were more like a to-do list of what we would accomplish each year. As I think back on this, I realize what a waste of time this was. Our annual objectives were something we did because our annual performance reviews – and thus our annual pay and bonus – were based on them. There was no allowance for not achieving any of the objectives, with the rationale during the review process (with ratings on a curve) being that someone who had achieved all of their objectives was a better performer than someone who hadn't. So, none of our objectives were particularly challenging or motivating; we created our objectives in such a way as to enable us to receive the best possible performance rating.

Setting objectives in this way will never develop outstanding performers, much less leaders. We don't learn and grow if we're not stretched; we need tough, we need demanding, we need to be pushed outside our comfort zones. This really doesn't happen often enough and this is why mediocrity persists throughout B2B marketing. It's why we so quickly latch onto the latest and greatest technology, tool or tactic as 'proof' of our effort and performance, because we have our SMART to-do list and at some fundamental level we don't actually know what we're trying to achieve, for ourselves as marketers or for our organizations.

In fairness, many of our organizations – especially larger ones – do include behavioural objectives. But too often these behavioural objectives are not aligned closely enough to our roles, our progression or our individual ambitions.

This is the ultimate responsibility of our leadership, to create the next generation of leaders within our marketing function. Yet the ways in which we set objectives within our organizations – and as a result, the ways in which we reward our people – don't allow for the types of learning and growth that create leaders.

What's professionally hardest and most uncomfortable? What will stretch our marketing abilities and push us outside our comfort zones? The answers to these questions will be different for each of us, but I can guarantee it won't have anything to do with a technical marketing skill or specific marketing output.

Including leadership objectives – appropriate to the level – would be enlightening; we just may learn and do some things that we never knew were possible, and in the process, become not only better marketers, but leaders of marketing.

Customer engagement for the social era

10

For better or worse, social media has forever and fundamentally changed our lives, both professionally and personally. It doesn't matter whether we are 'digital natives' or are old enough to remember a time before the internet, social media's impact on how we connect and communicate will continue to influence the world in which we live and work.

A mere five years ago, B2B marketers were just beginning to talk about social media as a 'game-changer'. We can debate the relative merits and metrics of its use, but today most of us have adopted social media to a greater or lesser extent as a platform and channel within our wider B2B marketing activity. The best among us have integrated social media successfully as a part of what we do as B2B marketers.

We know that our customer dynamic has changed and customers now control their buying journey. Our customers are more connected, more empowered and more knowledgeable, and they have a lot more choice.

As businesses – and as B2B marketers – there's such pressure to be 'on' social media at the moment that I worry we're not giving enough thought to what we're actually doing there and why. Because, ironically, even with all the noise and focus on social media, and the pervasiveness of social media 'experts' who are supposedly helping us to do social correctly, we are continuing to push out our sales and marketing messages via social channels just like we've always done through the so-called traditional channels. For example, we still create ads; we just place them on Facebook and LinkedIn and 'sponsor' content. And we still receive 'cold calls', but through direct messages now instead of the telephone.

Surely, we can do better than this.

Six rules for social engagement

My six rules for engaging customers through social media channels aren't intended to be a 'how to' guide for social media; we have more than enough of those already. But as I've been considering how and why we should be using social media for our B2B marketing activity, I've found we continually need to be aware of the following six things if we are to become more effective marketers in what is a social era.

Rule 1: Start by listening

I like to think of social media conversations as those you might have at a party. Just like at a party, you wouldn't announce your arrival at the door, nor would you join a group already having a discussion and jump in with what you wanted to talk about. Instead, you'd wander around a bit, grab a drink and then perhaps you'd join a group where there's a discussion that appears interesting. You'd spend some time, perhaps on the fringes of the group at first, listening to the conversation that's going on around you. After a while you might join in, with a question, a comment or an opinion.

Social media conversations are not very different – in order to understand what's important to our customers and thus better enable engagement that's meaningful to them, we really need to actively listen.

I don't think we're doing this very well in B2B. Do you remember the Peanuts comic strip by Charles M Schulz? There's one that I've always loved. In the first frame, Lucy asks Charlie Brown, 'So, what do you think?' In the next frame, Charlie Brown looks really grumpy and answers, 'What does it matter? You never listen anyways.' Lucy looks offended and responds (I imagine quite indignantly), 'I was just trying to make conversation.' He then tells her, 'When you make conversation, you have to listen too!' Lucy looks taken aback and finally exclaims, 'You do?'

This is a very old cartoon, yet it certainly reflects the current state of an awful lot of B2B social media interactions, even with the so-called social media experts.

We forget that the real purpose of social media for brands is to engage with our customers in meaningful ways in order to build relationships. We build relationships through ongoing interactions and conversations, and conversations mean listening.

When I was first starting to get my wider business involved with social media, I had a Twitter discussion with a self-styled social media guru who had written a blog that claimed that listening wasn't a strategy. The crux of the blog was that it was time to stop listening and start doing. And, I agreed, unless you want to be invisible on social media, at some point you do have to start actively participating in the conversation.

However, listening to our customers is fundamental to any business strategy, and I wanted some clarification about the blog's point of view. I asked this social media guru if they might advocate listening as a way to get started for those who were unsure how to begin on social media. The response was – and this is verbatim – if you're not already on social media, listening is the least of your problems.

That sure was a conversation-stopper.

I was trying to understand and learn, and this person was more interested in expounding upon their own point of view instead of listening to what really mattered to me. Even more interesting, I very well could have been a potential customer of this person (they were the head of a social media agency).

Needless to say, I quickly unfollowed that particular person and I'm still telling this story.

My point then – and now – is that the B2B world is still only at the beginning of getting to grips with social media. We are a long way behind our colleagues in B2C marketing and it's ironic, because we should be better at it than they are. B2B is fundamentally about building relationships, and social media presents such an opportunity to do so. Those of us in B2B marketing already know that all these interactions are going on out there on social platforms – with or without us – and we are already participating to a greater or lesser extent. But across our organizations there is not yet a real understanding of the power of social media in building the kinds of relationships that are so important for us as individuals and for our companies. There are still many people across our businesses who don't see the value these conversations bring or the impact they have in the context of the work they do.

Rule 2: Stop pushing, please

This social era means that we must look at all our marketing activities through a completely different lens from we did before. No matter what we do, we have to ask ourselves a critical question: Does this matter to our customers?

This social era is not about us, it's about our customers. And there's a clue in the word: social. One of the definitions for the word in the dictionary is 'relating to or designed for activities in which people meet each other'. Social media is a platform where people meet; when people meet there is an interaction and an exchange of value, for everyone involved in that exchange.

Just this week I saw a tweet from a marketing agency: Find out what our clients are saying about [us]!

Well, why should I care?

Social media isn't intended as and shouldn't be a one-way broadcast channel that we use to push out information and messages about ourselves; it's a two-way (and often multi-way) interaction with our customers. Continually pushing out our own content does not necessarily stimulate interaction; in fact, as I illustrated in my listening rule with the Twitter guru who completely alienated me, pushing can often be conversation-stoppers.

Too many of us in B2B marketing are still using social media as simply another channel through which to push out our marketing content, or as a means to drive our customers to our websites, without giving real thought to if and why that content will matter to our customers.

Furthermore, everything is content, every tweet, every post, every image, every like and share. It's all content, even if it's B2B. Our customers are becoming increasingly savvy about ignoring and even blocking what's not relevant or interesting to them.

We have only to consider programmatic marketing and the rise of ad blocking. Programmatic marketing is seen as the future of advertising on the web; essentially, it's the automation of advertising in real time, for the opportunity to show an ad to a specific customer, in a specific context. It happens as we navigate the web, no matter where we are. From our marketing perspective, programmatic may be easier, more flexible and more targeted, but we need to remember that it's still advertising, and it's still push marketing. Thus, programmatic has led to the rise of ad blocking, technology that we – and our customers – use to literally block ads from anywhere we may be online.

Depending upon our industry, we may not actually do much advertising per se. But the entire debate around programmatic and ad blocking is an interesting one, because it's essentially a debate about content and what content our customers are interested in and will engage with. People aren't blocking ads, they're blocking an unwanted experience, an intrusion or an annoyance.

This is unfortunate, because it's a lost opportunity. Serendipity is the chance or random occurrence of something in a happy or beneficial way.

It's essential to discovery, and part of what's wonderful about social media is the opportunity to discover the new. Yet in our quest to provide ongoing relevance we use technology based on algorithms and filters that mostly expose us to what we've already done, to what we already know and to people who think just like us. Just because something was of interest to us yesterday doesn't necessarily mean we will find it of interest today.

What this all means for B2B marketers is that we need to consider the impact of what we do on the audience we are trying to engage with. No matter our approach, if it feels 'pushy', it will be ignored and may well impact how our brands are more broadly perceived.

Rule 3: The 'So-What' factor

The 'So-What' factor is about being memorable and standing out from the competition. But we want to stand out for the right reasons. To our customers, the vast majority of B2B companies are all the same. We make the same claims about our products and services – the same benefits, the same solutions, the same features, the same pricing.

We need to do and be much more if we are going to be truly memorable, and one of the ways we can do this is through the value we bring through our social media interactions. This doesn't mean what we think is of value, it must be of value to our customers.

I've said it many times, but I'm going to say it again because in B2B we still don't get it: we as marketers are still too focused on ourselves and our organizations, about what we want to say and what's important or interesting to us.

Very simply, we need to stop talking about what we sell. Even our salespeople need to stop talking about what we sell. Yet we all come up against the same roadblock – if we can't talk about our products and services, what do we have to talk about with our customers?

We can start by understanding and then focusing on the big issues our customers are dealing with every day and talking about the ideas we have for confronting and dealing with these big issues. This is where real innovation within our companies can be found – in the ways in which our people think.

Campaigns and other marketing activities that are led by ideas – instead of led by products or services – are much more memorable because ideas engage people. This is hard for our organizations, because ideas are risky. But ultimately, if we can tap into those burning issues that consume our customers and are aligned with what we actually do sell, we will be better able to get past the 'So-What' factor.

Rule 4: Be responsive

Relationships are the heart of B2B and they are core to the social media experience, so we need to get better at having interactions with our customers that develop over time. This means being responsive to the conversations we participate in.

But being responsive is not the same as responding.

I continue to be interested in how words impact how we think and behave, and I turned to my dictionary again to find the definitions for respond and responsive:

- To **respond** means to supply an answer; in this context, it most often means from one's own point of view.
- Being **responsive** is defined as responding readily and with interest, implying receptiveness, understanding and empathy.

These two behaviours in the context of social media are at opposite ends of the spectrum.

We forget that the purpose of social media is to engage with our customers and build relationships through conversations, and conversations mean listening to and being responsive to our customers.

We're not doing this very well in B2B.

Let's go back to that Twitter exchange I used in my listening rule, where I was trying to understand more about using Twitter and asked a question of a social media expert. While this person certainly responded to my query, they weren't at all responsive to what I was actually saying. That kind of response negatively impacted my perception of that company – not just the person – to the extent that I continue to use it as an example of how too many agencies fundamentally don't understand the challenges we are facing in B2B.

This difference between 'respond' and 'responsive' is a big one in social media and it profoundly impacts the kinds of conversations we have and the relationships we develop, not to mention the perceptions our customers have of our brands.

We have to remember that we are no longer in control of the conversation, our customers are.

Rule 5: Just do it and keep on doing it!

Social media is for the long term. Like any relationship, social media relationship-building takes time and effort, and our efforts don't always translate into immediate results. It feels hard – even risky – when we're doing something we've never done before. Yet often what's hardest is the most rewarding.

In 2014, I started integrating social media into my marketing strategy, and it was actually the younger members of my team who pushed me into doing it. No one else in my company was doing much with social media at the time, although the central online team was championing its use. We didn't have any 'best practice' elsewhere in the company to show us the way and there were no corporate guidelines.

Moreover, I have to admit, I was extremely sceptical about the value of social media in a B2B corporate environment. Back then I just couldn't get my head around it; I mean, I was on Facebook and I had a LinkedIn profile, but I didn't actually use either one of them. And Twitter! What could anyone say in 140 characters that could possibly have any relevance or meaning to our customers? I really didn't get it at all. But my team convinced me we had to try, and two of the younger members went off to develop a plan.

A week or so later they came back to me with a really nice plan to implement social media activity over a period of eight months, with specific milestones and what looked like easy enough targets to achieve. We actually started out with just one tweet a day! We set targets for the number of followers and the rate of growth, and we agreed what was essentially a template that each of us would follow to ensure aligned tone of voice. At the time, the number of followers was the only metric we had, and growing that number was the only real objective. I wasn't sure then how it fitted into my overall marketing strategy, but it was a Plan. And since I was pretty clueless, I said great, go make it happen!

So, we just did it, and in less than a month we had achieved every milestone and target in that eight-month plan. Looking back, I now realize how much we really didn't know, but without us even being aware of it, social media quite quickly became a part of our 'day job'. We found that it wasn't all that hard and it didn't take a lot of time. In fact it was fun; we were actually engaging with our customers. We weren't all that great at it in the beginning; we pretty much made it up as we went along. But, we listened and we learned, we made ourselves visible and we were patient, and interestingly we found that we started to think differently, to think more about what was important to the people we were trying to engage with, in other words, our customers and what really mattered to them. And we got better at it over time.

Social media has now become pervasive throughout most of our personal lives, and for me, it's an ongoing and integral part of my professional as well as personal life. I'm truly in awe of the power of social media, the value these interactions bring and the impact they have for both individuals and businesses.

Rule 6: Quality not quantity

One of the many great quotes attributed to Steve Jobs is: 'Be a yardstick of quality. Some people aren't used to an environment where excellence is expected.'

Let's face it, there's an awful lot of mediocre marketing activity going on out there. We seem to live in a world where quantity is the measure of value and more is always better. We're always so busy, pushing out more and more content, implementing more activity, and hoping that some of it sticks. We always try to do more, primarily because we're measured by the quantity of the output instead of the quality of the outcome.

> Shouldn't we be thinking more about what's really worth marketing?

Quality needs to become an imperative for our marketing. It should surpass quantity every time. We need to start doing far fewer things, but do them to the very highest standard, and we need to agree that standard throughout the organization. Good enough is no longer good enough any more. This may mean having some difficult conversations with parts of our businesses. We may need to stop doing those activities that aren't providing the outcomes our business requires. We may need to stop supporting other parts of our business altogether.

Quality is thus ultimately about making choices on where we focus our attention, and therefore where we place our time and our budgets.

In the context of social media, quality is about the type of the interactions we have, the relationships we build and the engagement we create.

In particular, we've become too caught up in the social media numbers themselves as equating to the quality of what we're doing. We've become fixated on the number of followers we have instead of the engagement we achieve, in the same manner as we're obsessed with the number of visits to our websites. We should be focusing on those fewer connections who actually follow, read, share and talk about us in meaningful ways rather than the thousands upon thousands who connect with us once and then disappear.

On top of that, we often don't even get the tactical basics right; I continue to see poorly written content with grammatical errors and spelling mistakes for which there's simply no excuse.

Taking a big idea to market

How do we engage our B2B customers? How is it different from our competitors? Are there ways through which we can better know our customers and have discussions that will lead to a commercial opportunity?

Big ideas have the power to make a big impact. It's our ideas that ultimately separate us from our competitors in B2B and it's these ideas that have the power to create lasting customer engagement.

In this section, I'm going to walk you through a campaign I developed a few years ago that continues to make an impact, not just because it enabled the company to enter a new market but more importantly because it showed the business that a new way of delivering marketing activity could create benefits long after the campaign was over. This campaign won two prestigious marketing awards in 2014 and even though it's now been a few years since that campaign ended, I'm still asked to talk about it because it reflects a different way of thinking, doing and being for marketers.

Creating the big idea

This should sound familiar to many of you. One of the senior salespeople in the business came to me very excited and said, 'We're writing an amazing piece of thought leadership, and it will be ready for you to publish next month!'

The core idea actually was terrific. As we all know, anniversaries are great hooks for marketing. In the run-up to the 65th birthday of the foundation of the NHS, the business wanted to talk about what the NHS could and should look like in 10 years' time, on its 75th birthday. This was an important debate in the market at the time because in 2012 the government had passed the Health and Social Care Act; the NHS was operating under unprecedented budgetary constraint while in the midst of massive institutional reform.

These market conditions presented new opportunities for our business beyond where we had traditionally played. But when I sat down with the business to understand what they really wanted to achieve with this piece of 'thought leadership', I quickly realized there was simply no way a traditional thought leadership publication could achieve their objectives. Primary among those objectives was entry into a new market space where they needed to build awareness and credibility, and engage with different people – influencers and decision-makers – in the sector, not the usual finance people.

With such big ambitions, I saw the opportunity for marketing to do something very different from what we'd always done. We decided to turn our marketing process on its head – instead of a traditional 'push' campaign, from its inception we envisioned a multi-channel customer engagement campaign, driven by social media, where we could have open discussions and debate on not only the drivers and barriers for a future shared vision but the practical steps necessary to get there. We also wanted to bring the public voice into the debate. The campaign would then culminate in a more traditional report that we could take to our customers to stimulate buyer conversations that would align with our service offering.

What this meant was that we had to really understand our purpose and objectives for the campaign – who we wanted to engage with, where they were having the relevant conversations and, most importantly, what would inspire them to get involved in the story we wanted to create, enabling a campaign that would make a bigger impact and provide benefits long after the campaign ended.

From the outset, the foundation and focus of the campaign became about engaging on a very personal and emotional level, reminding people about what we cherish in the NHS and celebrating the eight decades of its achievements before getting into the very difficult discussions about what needed to be done differently.

Serendipitously, I had recently seen the IBM centennial film whose concept was around connecting the IBM technology over 100 years to the people who made it happen and the impact it had in the wider world. This IBM film inspired the short creative film that became the foundation for our campaign – the stories of ordinary people and their experiences with the NHS over the eight decades of its existence. The primary aim of the film was to drive people through social media channels to our website, where they could share their thoughts, ideas and experiences, and contribute to the developing story.

We continued to do our traditional marketing activity as well. The big difference was that we integrated everything under the campaign banner. For example, we still sponsored some conferences, but we made much more strategic choices about these events and were more creative around how we engaged with conference delegates – holding fringe events, roundtables and workshops around the emerging themes.

Five top tips for developing a big idea

The campaign was wildly successful, far exceeding every expectation as well as metric we had for it. By engaging upfront with a broad range of stakeholders and the general public on an issue that really mattered to them, the campaign enabled a different kind of conversation to develop that would not have been possible with a more traditional approach. Furthermore, at a time when B2B organizations were struggling to get to grips with new technology and new tactics, the campaign embraced social media as a primary channel for communication and engagement. By doing so, the campaign proved that social media can increase the impact of marketing campaigns within a B2B environment.

I personally learned five powerful lessons that remain highly relevant to B2B marketers today.

Lesson 1: Make it human

I continue to give presentations in both public and private forums to B2B marketers about what made this campaign an award-winning one. Without fail, in the Q&A following the presentation, someone always remarks that it was easy for me because the NHS and healthcare are highly emotional topics that everyone can relate to and their own particular markets are just not that emotional.

I come down hard on this perspective – it's lazy thinking and lazy marketing. Our job as marketers is to find that emotional connection with our customers, and then to create content and deliver campaigns that resonate and connect on that very personal, human level.

Think about it: how is it possible to make an emotional connection to a phone or a fizzy drink? The B2C marketing world has discovered how to tap into the human element of what they do. But it takes work and it takes knowing our customers on a much deeper level than as solely buyers of our products or services.

For the NHS campaign, there were many emotions which I could have capitalized on, but we found that the emotion that really connected with people was pride, and this emotion became the starting point for everything we did. The first time we showed the film, to an audience of over 100 senior people across the healthcare industry, when it ended, they cheered. It almost made me cry. A nursing association and an ambulance service asked for copies of the film to show within their own organizations at away days and the like. This is the kind of outcome that simply can't be measured or upon which we can put a price.

We are humans, engaging with humans. Let's make our marketing human as well.

Lesson 2: We must become social businesses

A social business is most commonly described as one that's been created and designed to address a social need, such as homelessness or poverty. But in the context of B2B marketing I use this term to describe a business that's completed the journey from an inside-out perspective to one that's outside-in, where the company culture and organizational behaviour begin and end with the customer.

If we are to truly embrace the customer in B2B, we must become social businesses, because the world is a fundamentally social place. I'm not just talking about social media here. Ever since we lived in caves, we've come together in social groups to live our lives, to collaborate and to share. As humans, we *are* social beings.

Social media has given us some extraordinary new ways to connect and interact with others. What started out as an important social tool has become an important business tool as well. But embedding social within our wider B2B businesses has been problematic. Granted, a lot more of our people have been getting involved with social media. But the majority still remain sceptical and even fearful of using it. It's no wonder really; much of B2B is highly risk averse, and social media *feels* risky.

So, we do social media training and create guidelines. We conduct social media 'boot camps' throughout our organizations, and many of us also have social media mentoring programmes. All with the objective of getting our people 'on' social media so they can become 'advocates' of our brands and help 'push out' our content.

But this is marketing's objective for social within our B2B organizations. It's the wrong perspective and it's why we're struggling. Embedding social into our businesses is about more than getting our people to use social media and it's not about creating employee advocates. It's about fundamentally changing our perspective, from thinking about what's important to us – as marketers – to what's important to our people, and most importantly, why it matters.

This is now the way in which our business world works, and we need to do a much better job helping our people at all levels in the organization understand the purpose of social, the Why for doing it. This simply cannot be done with slide deck presentations and mentoring by young people who admittedly totally 'get' social but don't always know how to ask the larger questions:

- Why should our people push out our content anyway?
- What's in it for them?
- How does it help them do their jobs better?
- Or become more employable over time?
- How do we better align the personal and professional (because that line has become extremely blurred in social)?
- What do they want to achieve with social media?
- What's the bigger picture here, for them?

It's not enough to just 'do' social. Simply being an employee advocate of our brands is not enough of a reason to get our people to embrace social. There must be a purpose to it, otherwise it's just more *stuff* continually being shoved out into a way overcrowded world.

In the context of my NHS campaign, this is where I first learned the power of social media itself for B2B marketing. Because when I was developing the social media elements of the campaign, I was continuously told that our customers didn't use social media. Well, they did, and we proved it. But we could have done even better.

Compared to the number of people throughout the company, we really had just a handful of people who were proactive with social media for the campaign. We could have done so much more on other platforms as well – for example on LinkedIn, on Instagram or with blogging. Even though the campaign achieved beyond our wildest expectations, how much more could we have achieved if significantly more people at all levels throughout the business had actively participated in the social elements of the campaign?

One of the many highlights of the campaign was when one of our most important customers tweeted a photo of our publication sitting right next to the top industry journal with the caption 'A must-read!' The inference, of course, was that our publication was as important as the journal that was read by every senior person in the industry.

Getting the companies we work for to embrace the use of social media remains a big challenge in B2B.

Five tips for getting the business you work for to become more social

1. Develop individual **clarity**: for each person, what do they want to achieve with their social media activity? What is their purpose? Do they want to use social media as a way of networking within their industry, connect with potential customers, participate in debate on issues, share industry or other news, or become a thought leader or influencer? Helping individuals or teams gain clarity on what they want to achieve is critical to building a meaningful social presence.
2. Work with **individuals**: forget workshops with a roomful of people and slide deck presentations, spend time with individuals – help them to:
   - choose which platforms they will use based on their purpose (I recommend LinkedIn and Twitter, which can be complementary);
   - write their profile;
   - find the right people to follow and the hash tags that are most relevant for them.

   Have them take two weeks to just 'listen', to understand what their customers are talking about on social platforms. Ask them to re-tweet and Favourite a lot; people love being re-tweeted and Favourited and it's one way to build followers.
3. Create small **teams of five**: each person to take ownership of a **'Twitter Day'** of the week. This means that in the beginning a different person each day of the week is responsible for tweeting and the other four can simply re-tweet that person. It takes a lot of the initial perceived time pressure off the individuals.

4 Create weekly **'Tweet Sheets'**: the marketing team can develop these not just for specific campaigns but for big issues that are in the news. These are particularly useful for individuals who are just starting, as it can be excruciatingly painful and time-consuming to communicate in a mere 140 characters – especially for a consultant!

5 The **20/20/20** rule: build an hour a day into their daily schedules (20 minutes in the morning, at lunchtime and at the end of the day). This is enough to begin to build a solid social presence. A critical factor for social success is committing to a schedule and sticking to it.

Social media is more than marketing's job within the organization; it's everyone's job. Until we can extend our social media engagement activity beyond the marketing function into our businesses and throughout our organizations, we are not going to be able to realize the full potential that social can bring to our wider B2B marketing activity.

Lesson 3: Captivate the wider business upfront

Critical to the success of the campaign was the work we did getting the wider business invested in the campaign from the start. But I have to admit this happened almost by accident.

Because I had a really tiny budget, with the exception of the film, we had to completely develop and implement the campaign in-house, and this meant gaining wide commitment from the business to harness the time, talent and energy of our people outside the marketing function to deliver many elements of the campaign.

We created a campaign project team which included people of all levels within the business. In addition to owning and contributing to elements of the campaign, this team became the campaign 'champions' throughout the business, gaining high levels of internal engagement, excitement and involvement in the marketing activity. We actually had people of all levels throughout the business itself coming to the marketing team asking to work on the campaign!

The campaign ultimately became a real collaboration between marketing, sales and other functions across the business, with little or no delineation between what marketing did and what the business did, and became an extraordinary experience for everyone involved.

Lesson 4: Take some risks

We took a lot of risks with the campaign because we did many things that had never been done within the organization. Chief among these risks was that this single campaign was the only marketing activity we did for the whole year for this part of the business. We poured the entire sector budget into this campaign, which meant we had to stop doing a lot of other marketing activity we typically did for the business over the course of the year.

Instead of starting with publishing a thought leadership report from our own point of view, and only then developing a marketing campaign around that report, we engaged upfront with stakeholders to debate the issues and articulate a shared vision. We eventually published a report, but we did so a full eight months after we began the campaign.

The film was a pivotal element of the campaign as it set the tone for what followed. Instead of creating a talking-heads video of our subject-matter experts speaking to camera, we developed a creative, emotionally driven film that tapped into the very real emotions of ordinary people. We even used some of our staff in the film.

We launched the campaign with only two pieces of content: the film and a single webpage with minimal copy, and then developed much of the campaign and its content in real time, by being responsive to the conversations across social media, online and in the market.

What was riskiest, though, was that we were asking people to get involved. Because even though we had a clear line of sight internally into what we wanted to sell into the market, the campaign wasn't about us or what our organization did, it was about a big issue with far-reaching impact. It could have been a disaster, no one might have responded and it all might have been just one more piece of noise out in the market. Understanding the risks and being open about them was our way of mitigating those risks.

Lesson 5: What comes next?

We became so caught up in delivering the campaign, so much of it in real time, over such an extensive period of time, that we didn't give any thought to what we were going to do next. As a result, we lost momentum, both in the market and within our organization. We simply forgot that one of the essential ingredients of a great story is having a great ending that keeps our customers wanting more.

This isn't really surprising. Most B2B companies struggle with articulating any story beyond what they sell. As marketers, we become so consumed with what we do at a functional level in the moment that we simply don't think long term.

The biggest lesson I learned that keeps on informing all of my B2B marketing activity is that we need to work harder and get better at developing interlinking, ongoing stories and programmes that align with both our business and our purpose. These stories then become the thread that joins up all our sales and marketing activity, and gives us a much a clearer and more compelling voice in the market.

Being different in B2B marketing 11

CASE STUDY Volvo's Live Test series

For me, the most creative, stand-out B2B campaign of all time has to be Volvo's. I'm sure everyone has now seen the 2013 YouTube video of Jean-Claude Van Damme doing the splits between two massive trucks reversing down a motorway at dawn.

I once silenced a room full of very senior salespeople with this *Epic Split* video. Complete and utter silence. Which led into a presentation I did for that group of salespeople about sales and marketing working together.

What this video did was capture a moment of such awe and beauty that it resonated far beyond its truck buyers. And without once 'selling' us on features and benefits, it reflected the stunning precision and performance of its trucks, which are intrinsic elements of its brand. What we tend to forget, though, is that this 75-second video was merely one in a series of short films that were part of a long-running campaign – a much wider and very traditional B2B launch campaign for Volvo's new fleet of five mega-trucks.

Volvo trucks make up more than two-thirds of the Volvo Group's portfolio and they estimate that approximately 15 per cent of all food in Europe is delivered by a truck from the Volvo Group (Annual Report, 2015). Their trucks also transport furniture, clothing, computers and many other products that most people need and use in their daily lives. They are classic B2B.

In 2012 Volvo was undergoing a major shift. They had put in place a new business strategy, begun an intense phase of renewing their product portfolios, initiated a new 'Brand Positioning Project, which was a key part of the Volvo Group's growth strategy' (Annual Report, 2012), and were launching their new fleet of mega-trucks – their first major product launch in 20 years.

The Live Test series of YouTube videos was created to demonstrate the specific capabilities of these massive trucks, and to appeal to truck buyers as well as the organizations they drove for. There were six films in all:

- *The Ballerina* features the world-record-holding high-liner walking across a wire between two speeding trucks to demonstrate precision handling.
- In *The Technician*, a Volvo truck drives over the head of an engineer buried up to his neck in sand in order to demonstrate the 12-inch clearance between ground and undercarriage.
- The strength of the front towing hook is showcased in *The Hook*, with Volvo Trucks president Claes Nilsson standing on the end of a truck suspended 66 feet above a wind-swept harbour in Gothenburg, Sweden.
- *The Hamster* illustrates the sensitivity and control of the steering system, with Charlie the hamster steering a truck up a rough quarry road.
- *The Chase* features manoeuvrability, with one of these huge trucks winding through the streets of an old Spanish city chased by a herd of bulls.
- And the final film, *The Epic Split*.

Volvo had big aspirations – they wanted the whole world talking about their trucks. And wow, the world talked! Between 2012 and 2014 the Live Test series of films had over 100 million views on YouTube and were shared 8 million times. The series went on to win every major award in the industry, including the Cannes Lions Creative Marketer of the Year in 2014, followed by Grand Prix Lions for Creative Effectiveness in 2015. The first award is one of the most coveted awards in marketing and advertising. The latter prize measures how a campaign has met or exceeded the campaign objectives over time. Unlike the other categories, the effectiveness award includes campaigns spanning a multi-year period and focuses on results – both quantitative and qualitative.

A critical element in the development of the campaign was how the upfront research substantially informed the creative. Further, ongoing conversations between the creative teams and the engineering teams inspired many of the ideas for the films, significantly impacting the very nature of what they ended up producing. They didn't just look at the new trucks' product features and benefits; they looked at how they all actually worked and what made them different.

The creative team also looked deeply into both the buyers and the users. The big surprise of the research was the incredibly strong emotional connection between the truck drivers and their trucks. Who could have imagined that a truck would provoke such strong attachments from their drivers? This emotional element then became a central focus of the films. The second surprise of their research was the sheer number of people who had an influence on the buying decision – from the drivers themselves, to their friends, families, colleagues, bosses, and even the businesses whose products their trucks carry.

This is a real learning point for us in B2B marketing – the Volvo creative team didn't have any preconceptions about what their research would tell them. And they didn't just rely on the data; they spoke to people, to the engineers who built the trucks and to the drivers themselves.

Volvo has continued the campaign with the December 2015 release on YouTube of *Look Who's Driving*. This two-and-a-half-minute film features a full-size truck, a four-year-old girl with a remote control and a gravel pit filled with obstacles. It's funny and quirky, yet at the same time it demonstrates the toughness and mobility of its trucks. It's already had 12 million views and counting, and, like its predecessors, is supported by ongoing 'traditional' marketing activity.

Beyond the awareness of the YouTube views and shares, the Live Test series has become arguably the most talked about product launch film in B2B.

What B2B marketers can learn from Volvo

What's of most interest to me as a B2B marketer is that Volvo started with a 'Big Idea' that was so much greater than the products they were selling. While the content they created is aligned to those products, what they are doing is 'selling' us on the brand itself. These were not little videos full of product features, narrated by 'talking heads', they featured real people in interesting and unusual situations.

Furthermore, upon winning the Cannes Lions Creative Effectiveness award, Lars Terling, Vice President of Marketing and Communication at Volvo Trucks, made a profound comment that should remain an object lesson for all B2B marketers:

> The Live Test campaign proves it is possible to generate global impact even in a business-to-business environment like ours. This is a result of... creative minds and having the courage to do something new and different. (Forsman & Bodenfors, 2015)

Being B2B marketers

Why are we B2B marketers? Why did we enter the profession in the first place? Some of us may have ended up here by chance or through good luck, but the majority of us made a conscious decision to go into B2B marketing. Do we remember why? We may have been seduced by the technology or the tactics, but I suspect we saw opportunity, the opportunity for marketing to be different in markets that had not fundamentally changed in a very long time.

These past few years, though, we've been under a lot of pressure. As our products and services become ever more undifferentiated and all the information our customers may have ever wanted now lies a click away, our organizations want and expect marketing to provide far more than ever before, but with a lot fewer resources. In too many cases, that 'more' isn't even actually clearly expressed, but – in marked contrast to the previous decade – we're now expected to actively report on marketing performance and deliver results.

Do we know what results we are supposed to deliver? A majority of us will answer that question with one word: leads. Because leads are what feed sales and sales delivers revenue, and revenue is what our organizations' leadership care about.

At least, that's what we've been led to believe.

This is the third and final overriding fallacy of our time, that marketing serves this singular, core purpose, to feed sales.

In Part Three, I've argued that while lead generation is a part of what marketing does, it's not our core purpose. It's distracting us from fulfilling our promise within our organizations and dismisses our potential to contribute to the wider business dialogue. This focus on lead generation has led us into a tactically led, short-term approach to marketing that we want to believe is strategic but is not. We are constantly reacting to our business demands instead of driving, influencing and shaping them.

I've also spent quite a bit of time on the 4Ps of the marketing mix and its iterations, as a means of widening our vision for B2B marketing and getting to grips with our purpose. As part of this rediscovery, I've argued that it's not insight we're lacking in B2B, but creativity. We make the excuse that B2B is boring, yet I've showcased case studies of well-known B2B brands whose creativity has made an impact far beyond their industries, enabling them to be very different from their competitors.

Moreover, I've looked at our B2B marketing individuals, teams and leadership and what we need to consider – the qualities, attributes, education and skills – if we are to *be different* and really create value within our organizations.

Finally, I've given some concrete examples from my own experience in B2B of making a bigger impact and delivering results that have been highly valued by both customers and the business. And no, they're not about lead generation at all.

Essential steps to *be different*

Change is difficult. There are always challenges and resistance, even from our leadership. For B2B marketing, change most likely won't happen quickly or easily. It may not even start with our marketing leadership. But change will happen and we can either drive it, be a part of it or be left behind. It is our choice.

That choice involves having absolute clarity on who we are and who we want to be as B2B marketers. If that involves going back to basics, learning and even relearning what this profession of ours is all about, then that is what we must do.

We must acknowledge that if we want to *be different*, we must *think* and *do different* as well. Like admitting we want change and being willing to do what it takes to embody that change. Like no matter what else is going on within our organizations, taking responsibility for becoming that change. Like making sure we learn not just the tactical skills, but the leadership skills we need for a different kind of marketing career success.

As I expressed at the beginning of this book, it all begins with strategy, strategy for marketing within our organizations, as well as ourselves as B2B marketers, that provides the direction for the change we envision. Strategy is our foundation for enabling that change, whether that's in our current organization, or the next, or the next.

Where do we start? Five habits to nurture

As with thinking and doing different, the first step is to make a conscious decision to be different. We can start by nurturing these five habits:

1. **No excuses:** Focus your attention on what you *can* do, not on what you can't. There will always be obstacles and those who prefer to maintain the status quo. Seek and provide clarity about what is possible, instead of what is impossible.
2. **Prioritize:** Start making choices about what marketing does and doesn't do; there will never be enough budget or buy-in or time. Concentrate on what's important instead of what's urgent. Only do those activities that provide the outcomes the business actually wants. Learn to say No.
3. **Be future-oriented:** Look towards the future, not the past. Have clarity for what you want to become. Be ruthless about what you personally need and what your team needs to do to get there.

4 **Have courage:** Be prepared to take risks. The new and different always involves risk, and risk means the possibility for failure. Do it anyway; the first step is always the hardest one. Start small but think bigger and be more. Better to beg forgiveness than ask for permission.

5 **Always be learning:** There is always something new to learn. Consistently make the time to learn something new and challenging, something that pushes you outside your comfort zone. Learn from those both within and outside your company – customers, competitors, those more junior as well senior to you.

Next steps: five questions and five actions

If we are to begin to *be different* we must continually ask tough questions of ourselves and those around us. I have explored many of these questions throughout Part Three, but the five questions and corresponding actions listed in Table 11.1 are an essential starting point.

Table 11.1 Be different Q&A

Five questions to ask	Five actions to take
Do I have a clear vision of who I want to be as a marketer? In other words, where am I today and where do I want to be tomorrow?	Plot your career path. This is not a list of job titles, these are the progressive outcomes you want to achieve in your career. Start with your own personal WHY. My 3D Marketing System, which I introduced in Chapter 5, is just as effective for individuals as it is for the marketing function.
Am I fluent in the fundamentals as well as the tactics and tools of my profession?	Perform a personal SWOT analysis. Understand your strengths and be brutally honest about the areas that you need to improve and what further knowledge you need.
What additional marketing qualifications or other learning do I need?	Your SWOT analysis will have highlighted those areas where further learning will be required. While the fashion of the moment may be to learn 'on the job', you will most likely have to go outside your organization for this learning. Do your research and take the courses or achieve the qualifications you need to be the marketer you want to be.

(*Continued*)

Table 11.1 *(Continued)*

Five questions to ask	Five actions to take
Have I learned something new lately?	Take on a new challenge. It can be anything and doesn't necessarily have to be related to work or to marketing. Even the attempt to become proficient at something new, especially if it takes you out of your comfort zone, will stimulate your thinking and your imagination.
Am I able to achieve what I want as a B2B marketer in this organization?	There may be too many things within your particular organization over which you have no influence or control. You may feel like marketing is going backwards instead of forwards. You may have a new boss who just doesn't 'get it' or there may be no real opportunity for progression. Your colleagues may not have the mindset or skills to be different. If that's the case, don't hesitate. Go somewhere else. Go somewhere you will be celebrated instead of merely tolerated. And do it now.

Conclusion

Being better B2B marketers

There's never been a more exciting time to be a B2B marketer. Of course, there's a tremendous amount of continuous change and the pace of that change often feels overwhelming. But when has work or life ever been without change?

To deal effectively with change, we must change; it's that simple. Change means opportunity – for both ourselves as individuals and for our B2B organizations – and as B2B marketers we can lead that change. But first we must acknowledge that we've been marketing under false assumptions, and adopting as truths three overriding marketing fallacies that are continuing to hinder our ability to make the kind of impact for our businesses that we crave.

There are more tactics and channels and technology than we have ever had to cope with before; and our customers are more knowledgeable, empowered and in control of the buying journey. Yet even though the marketing fundamentals remain the same, we are ignoring these foundations of our profession, continuing with a blinkered focus on the tactical elements of marketing, without the hard work that must be done first in order to be most effective.

We want marketing to be more strategic and have a greater impact for the business. But we are not always thinking, acting or being strategic, and too many of us don't know how. A marketing plan is not a marketing strategy; outputs are not outcomes; and tactics alone can't and won't produce the results our businesses want and need.

Yet those tactics do drive leads for sales, and we can measure (more or less) our contribution. So, we continue to believe that this is what our businesses want from us, without realizing that this focus will never change how our organizations perceive marketing.

Purpose-driven marketing

Ultimately, the purpose of marketing is to create an environment for business success. This definition of success won't be the same for all organizations; inevitably, there will be many layers to that definition. By purpose-driven marketing I mean merely that there must be a purpose for what we do as marketers; whether that's in large or small ways, it doesn't really matter, as long as we have clarity for why we are doing what we do.

The onslaught of digital technology has created a generation of marketers who simply don't know the difference between strategy and tactics, channels and content. This new generation, who call themselves 'digital marketers', are often guilty of thinking there is no value in and nothing to learn from what came before. Yet without this foundation in marketing theory and grounding in marketing principles, we will never understand how marketing fits within the wider business landscape, the relevance of how marketing has addressed the business challenges of the past, or why it's important. If we don't understand marketing's importance, then our organizations certainly never will. We will be left continually distracted by whatever is the latest fad, finding ourselves woefully unable to contribute to the sustainable success of our businesses.

Tactics are for the moment, ideas are forever

It's the compelling and lasting nature of ideas that has the potential to transform and differentiate what we do as marketers. These ideas have the power to create impact and meaning beyond what we do. And it's through ideas that we can engage with our customers in ways that build and maintain the relationships that sustain our B2B world.

Strategy is our foundation and this is where we must begin, with three fundamental questions that we must ask of all our B2B marketing activity:

- Why are we doing this?
- What do we want to achieve (for ourselves, our customers and our companies)?
- How does this matter?

Think different, do different, be different

I hope you've been challenged and inspired by what you've read throughout this book, and will be able to make use of some of the practical advice. I have one last challenge for you. No matter who you are, what organization you work for, or what level you are within your marketing team, I'd like each and every one of you to begin thinking just a little bit differently about what you do as a B2B marketer. Starting right now, think bigger, beyond marketing, in terms of the engagement you want to have with your customers instead of solely in terms of what your organization sells and irrespective of the latest tactics and technology. Ask yourself and ask others throughout your business: What is really important to our customers? What resonates with them on an emotional level? Which of their issues align with our products or services and where do we connect with them on these issues?

Then do one thing differently, one small thing that's even just a little bit different, one thing that feels a little bit risky. You may not get it quite right the first time, but you can try. You just might find you can be a different kind of marketer, one who doesn't just develop brochures for your salespeople, push 'stuff' out into the market or depend upon 'digital' as a marketing distribution channel to your customers. You have the opportunity to become the kind of marketer who enables your wider business to become memorable in the hearts and minds of your customers, creating the kind of engagement with your customers that builds lasting relationships, long after any sales promotion or marketing campaign is forgotten.

I'll leave you with one final thought. The 1989 film *Dead Poets Society*, starring Robin Williams as an English teacher in an all-boys prep school, made a major impact on the scriptwriter for Apple's 'Think Different' campaign, Rob Siltanen. For those not familiar with the film, it is fundamentally about changing perspectives and taking risks. There is a scene in the film where Williams stands on top of his desk during a lecture:

> Why do I stand up here? I stand upon my desk to remind myself that we must constantly look at things in a different way. You see the world looks very different up here.

He then has his students climb on to the desk; this scene particularly resonated with Siltanen and makes a fitting signature for this book:

> Just when you think you know something, you have to look at it in another way... Dare to strike out and find new ground.

REFERENCES AND FURTHER READING

Introduction

Davies, A (2015a) How to get sales to use your marketing content [blog], Salesforce, 10 September [Online] https://www.salesforce.com/blog/2015/09/how-to-get-sales-to-use-your-marketing-content.html [accessed 7 March 2017]

Davies, A (2015b) How to fix the $50bn problem in B2B content marketing [blog], Econsultancy, 3 September [Online] https://econsultancy.com/blog/66882-how-to-fix-the-50bn-problem-in-b2b-content-marketing/ [accessed 5 March 2017]

MacDonald, J in Morin, A (2014) The questions that should keep business leaders awake at night, *Forbes* [Online] https://www.forbes.com/sites/amymorin/2014/04/14/the-4-questions-that-should-keep-business-leaders-awake-at-night/ [accessed 18 March 2017]

Chapter 1

English. Oxford Living Dictionaries (2017) [Online] https://en.oxforddictionaries.com/ [accessed 7 March 2017]

Johnson, S (1998) *Who Moved My Cheese? An amazing way to deal with change in your work and in your life*, Vermilion, London

Lingqvist, O, Plotkin, C L and Stanley, J (2015) Do you really understand how your business customers buy? *McKinsey Quarterly*, February [Online] http://www.mckinsey.com/business-functions/marketing-and-sales/our-insights/do-you-really-understand-how-your-business-customers-buy [accessed 10 March 2016]

Plutchik, R (2001) The nature of emotions, *American Scientist*, **89** (4), p 344

The Guardian (2014) Maya Angelou quotes: 15 of the best, the *Guardian* [Online] https://www.theguardian.com/books/2014/may/28/maya-angelou-in-fifteen-quotes [accessed 18 March 2017]

Chapter 2

Adobe Digital Index (2016) Digital video benchmark report Q1 2016, Slideshare [Online] https://www.slideshare.net/adobe/adobe-digital-index-q1-2016-digital-video-benchmark-report [accessed 15 July 2016]

ALF Insight (2016) Marketing trends, spend & forecasts 2016 [Online] http://www.uploadlibrary.com/DigitalRadish/ALFINSIGHT_Marketing_2016.pdf [accessed 29 May 2017]

Ascend2 (2016) 2016 Leadership perspective on the state of digital marketing [Online] http://mktg.actonsoftware.com/acton/attachment/248/f-1c47/1/-/-/-/-/Ascend2_State%20of%20Digital%20Marketing_Marketing%20Leadership.pdf [accessed 29 May 2016]

Brenner, M (2016)100+ amazing marketing stats you need to know in 2016, Marketing Insider Group [Online] https://marketinginsidergroup.com/content-marketing/160-amazing-marketing-stats-you-need-to-know/ [accessed 3 December 2016]

Canada Post (2015) A bias for action: the neuroscience behind the response driving power of direct mail [Online] https://www.canadapost.ca/assets/pdf/blogs/CPC_Neuroscience_EN_150717.pdf [accessed 11 December 2016]

Content Marketing Institute (2016) 2016 Benchmarking report [Online] http://contentmarketinginstitute.com/wp-content/uploads/2015/09/2016_B2B_Report_Final.pdf [accessed 29 May 2017]

Content Marketing Institute (2017) [Online] http://contentmarketinginstitute.com/ [accessed 12 January 2016]

DemandWave (2016) 2016 State of B2B digital marketing [Online] http://go.demandwave.com/rs/306-MLQ-910/images/2016-State-of-B2B-Digital-Marketing.pdf [accessed 29 May 2017]

Economist Intelligence Unit (2016) The path to 2020: marketers seize the customer experience [Online] *The Economist* [Online] https://www.eiuperspectives.economist.com/sites/default/files/EIU_Thepathto2020_PDF.pdf [accessed 21 November 2016]

Econsultancy (2016) Email marketing industry census 2016 [Online] http://content.adestra.com/hubfs/2016_Reports_and_eGuides/2016-Email-Marketing-Industry-Census.pdf [accessed 29 May 2017]

English. Oxford Living Dictionaries (2017) [Online] https://en.oxforddictionaries.com/ [accessed 11 November 2016]

Gallo, A (2016) A refresher on marketing myopia, *Harvard Business Review* [Online] https://hbr.org/2016/08/a-refresher-on-marketing-myopia [accessed 11 March 2016]

Gardner, A (2010) The power of words [video], YouTube [Online] https://www.youtube.com/watch?v=QYcXTlGLUgE [accessed 12 January 2017]

Hubspot (2016) How to create personas [Online] https://knowledge.hubspot.com/contacts-user-guide-v2/how-to-create-personas [accessed 11 November 2016]

Levitt, T (1960) Marketing myopia, *Harvard Business Review*, **4** (4), pp 59–80 (reprinted July–August 2004)

Microsoft (2015) How does digital affect Canadian attention spans? *The Telegraph* [Online] http://www.telegraph.co.uk/science/2016/03/12/humans-have-shorter-attention-span-than-goldfish-thanks-to-smart/ [accessed 7 March 2017]

Pritchard, M (2013) Digital marketing exhibition and conference [Online] http://www.businessinsider.com/pg-proclaims-digital-marketing-is-dead-2013-9?IR=T [accessed 12 December 2016]

Regalix (2016) State of B2B marketing 2016 [Online] http://www.regalix.com/by_regalix/research/reports/state-of-b2b-marketing-2016/

Richardson, A (2010) Understanding customer experience, *Harvard Business Review* [Online] https://hbr.org/2010/10/understanding-customer-experie [accessed 12 December 2016]

Ritson, M (2016) Tactics without strategy is dumbing down our discipline, *Marketing Week*, 11 May [Online] https://www.marketingweek.com/2016/05/11/mark-ritson-beware-the-tactification-of-marketing/ [accessed 11 March 2016]

Salesforce Research (2016) 2016 State of marketing [Online] https://www.salesforce.com/uk/form/pdf/2016-state-of-marketing.jsp [accessed 23 July 2016]

SAS (2017) What is big data and why it matters [Online] https://www.sas.com/en_us/insights/big-data/what-is-big-data.html [accessed 7 March 2017]

Smith, N *et al* (2010) The new marketing myopia, *Journal of Public Policy & Marketing*, **29** (1), pp 4–11

Vizard, S (2016) Sir Martin Sorrell: 'Brands are starting to question if they have over-invested in digital', *Marketing Week*, 24 August [Online] https://www.marketingweek.com/2016/08/24/sir-martin-sorrell-brands-are-starting-to-question-if-they-have-over-invested-in-digital/

Chapter 3

Marketing Campaign Case Studies (2008) Think Different [blog] 3 May [Online] http://marketing-case-studies.blogspot.co.uk/2008/03/think-different-campaign.html [accessed 7 March 2017]

Siltanen, R (2011) The real story behind Apple's 'Think Different' campaign, *Forbes*, 14 December [Online] https://www.forbes.com/sites/onmarketing/2011/12/14/the-real-story-behind-apples-think-different-campaign/ [accessed 12 December 2016]

Chapter 4

B2B Marketing in association with Circle Research (2016) High performance B2B marketing 2016–17, June

Benioff, M (2016) Businesses are the greatest platforms for change, *Huffington Post* [Online] http://www.huffingtonpost.com/marc-benioff/businesses-are-the-greate_b_8993240.html [accessed 25 November 16]

Content Marketing Institute (2017a) 2017 B2B content marketing benchmark survey – North America [Online] http://contentmarketinginstitute.com/wp-content/uploads/2016/09/2017_B2B_Research_FINAL.pdf [accessed 18 March 2017]

Content Marketing Institute (2017b) 2017 B2B content marketing benchmark survey – UK [Online] http://contentmarketinginstitute.com/wp-content/uploads/2016/12/2017_UK_Research_FINAL.pdf [accessed 18 March 2017]

Drucker, P F (1963) Managing for business effectiveness, *Harvard Business Review* [Online] https://hbr.org/1963/05/managing-for-business-effectiveness [accessed 5 December 2016]

Drucker, P F (nd) Goodreads quotes [Online] http://www.goodreads.com/quotes/420819-if-you-want-something-new-you-have-to-stop-doing [accessed 8 December 2016]

Greenburg, P (2015) The clarity of definition: CRM, CE and CX. Should we care? ZDNet, 10 August [Online] http://www.zdnet.com/article/the-clarity-of-definition-crm-ce-and-cx-should-we-care/ [accessed 5 December 2016]

Havas Group (2017) Meaningful brands [Online] http://www.meaningful-brands.com/ [accessed 18 March 2017]

Kipling, R (1902) *Just So Stories: The elephant's child* [Online] http://www.kiplingsociety.co.uk/poems_serving.htm [accessed 5 December 2016]

Manning, H (2010) Customer experience defined [blog], Forrester, 23 November [Online] http://blogs.forrester.com/harley_manning/10-11-23-customer_experience_defined [accessed 5 December 2016]

Pontefract, D (2016) CEOs now believe their customers are expecting a higher sense of purpose, *Forbes*, 19 January [Online] http://www.forbes.com/sites/danpontefract/2016/01/19/ceos-now-believe-their-customers-are-expecting-a-higher-sense-of-purpose/#1890af3d625c [accessed 25 November 2016]

PwC (2016) Redefining business success in a changing world, PricewaterhouseCoopers [Online] https://www.pwc.com/gx/en/ceo-survey/2016/landing-page/pwc-19th-annual-global-ceo-survey.pdf [accessed 25 November 2016]

Sinek, S (2009) *Start with Why: How great leaders inspire everyone to take action*, Penguin Books, London, p 39

TEDx Puget Sound (2009) Simon Sinek: how great leaders inspire action [video], TEDx [Online] https://www.ted.com/talks/simon_sinek_how_great_leaders_inspire_action [accessed 7 December 2016]

Unilever (2017) Purpose, values and principles [Online] https://www.unilever.com/about/who-we-are/purpose-and-principles/ [accessed 4 January 2017]

Wartzman, R (2015) What Unilever shares with Apple and Google, *Forbes*, 7 January [Online] http://fortune.com/2015/01/07/what-unilever-shares-with-google-and-apple/ [accessed 25 November 2016]

Chapter 5

CEB and Google (2013) From promotion to emotion: connecting B2B customers to brands, CEB [Online] https://www.cebglobal.com/marketing-communications/b2b-emotion.html [accessed 18 March 2017]

Chapter 6

Contagious Magazine (2013) Contagious case study: Coca-Cola, *Contagious Magazine*, issue 32 [Online] http://contagious-com.s3.amazonaws.com/assets/images/Coke%20case%20study/Cokecasestudy32.pdf [accessed 8 January 2017]

Institute of Practitioners in Advertising (2013) Johnathan Mildenhall on creativity [video], YouTube [Online] https://www.youtube.com/watch?v=roTolLHJgOw [35:26] [accessed 8 January 2017]

Weed, K (2016a) Here's what won't change in marketing in 2017, *Marketing Week*, 6 December [Online] https://www.marketingweek.com/2016/12/06/keith-weed-column/ [accessed 11 December 2016]

Weed, K (2016b) Why I believe it's never been more important to put people at the heart of marketing [blog], LinkedIn, 6 December [Online] https://www.linkedin.com/pulse/why-i-believe-its-never-been-more-important-put-people-keith-weed [accessed 11 December 2016]

Chapter 7

B2M Marketing (2016) CXcellence: the B2B Conference 2016, London

Borden, NH (1964) The concept of the marketing mix, *Journal of Advertising Research*, pp 2–7 and reprinted in Baker, M J (ed) (2001) *Marketing: Critical perspectives on business and management*, vol 5, Routledge, London, pp 3–4

CEB and Google (2013) From promotion to emotion: connecting B2B customers to brands [Online] https://www.cebglobal.com/marketing-communications/b2b-emotion.html [accessed 18 March 2017]

Content Marketing Institute (2017a) 2017 B2B content marketing benchmark survey – North America [Online] http://contentmarketinginstitute.com/wp-content/uploads/2016/09/2017_B2B_Research_FINAL.pdf [accessed 18 March 2017]

Content Marketing Institute (2017b) 2017 B2B content marketing benchmark survey – UK [Online] http://contentmarketinginstitute.com/wp-content/uploads/2016/12/2017_UK_Research_FINAL.pdf [accessed 18 March 2017]

Converse, P D (1945) The development of the science of marketing: an exploratory survey, *Journal of Marketing*, **10** (1), July, pp 14–23

English. Oxford Living Dictionaries (2017) [Online] https://en.oxforddictionaries.com/ [accessed 16 March 2017]

IBM (2011) IBM centennial film: 100 X 100 – a century of achievements have changed the world [video], YouTube [Online] https://www.youtube.com/watch?v=39jtNUGgmd4 [accessed 10 February 2017]

IBM Singapore (2013) IBM Singapore 60/60 exhibit [video], YouTube [Online] https://www.youtube.com/watch?v=w0BpWnPWUVA [accessed 18 March 2017]

Jobber, D and Fahy, J (2003) *Foundations of Marketing*, McGraw-Hill, London

Kanter, R M (2011) How great companies think differently, *Harvard Business Review*, November [Online] https://hbr.org/2011/11/how-great-companies-think-differently

Kaye, K (2015) Tangled up in Big Blue: IBM replaces smarter planet with… Bob Dylan, *Advertising Age* [Online] http://adage.com/article/datadriven-marketing/ibm-replaces-smarter-planet-cognitive-business-strategy/300774/ [accessed 10 February 2017]

Lauterborn, B (1990) New marketing litany; four Ps passé; C-words take over, *Advertising Age*, 41, p 26

Marketo (2016) *Website and SEO for Lead Generation* [Online e-Book] https://uk.marketo.com/ebooks/website-and-seo-for-lead-generation/ [accessed 12 January 2017]

McCarthy, E J (1964) *Basic Marketing: A managerial approach*, Richard D Irwin, Homewood, IL

Schneider Electric (2015) Llama Superstar [Online video] https://www.youtube.com/watch?v=MfrPFc5mK3o) [accessed 9 February 2017]

Starkey, R (2016) 100 powerful B2B lead generation statistics [blog] Digital Stream Media, 2 June [Online] http://content.digitalmediastream.co.uk/blog/100-powerful-b2b-lead-generation-statistics [accessed 12 January 2017]

Van Vliet, V (2011) *Service marketing mix – 7 Ps* [Online] http://www.toolshero.com/marketing/service-marketing-mix-7ps [accessed 14 January 2017]

Weir, M (2016) Sales saturation: is your sales team getting soaked? [blog] LinkedIn, 21 January [Online] https://business.linkedin.com/marketing-solutions/blog/marketing-for-tech-companies/2016/sales-saturation--is-your-sales-team-getting-soaked- [accessed 18 March 2017]

Chapter 8

Brenner, M (2017) The ultimate guide to the best marketing conferences of 2017, *Marketing Insider Group*, 3 January [Online] https://marketinginsidergroup.com/strategy/best-marketing-conferences-2017/ [accessed 14 February 2017]

Covey, S (1989) *The 7 Habits of Highly Effective People*, Simon & Schuster, New York

Drucker, P F (1967; 2009) *The Effective Executive*, HarperCollins, New York

Drucker, P F (2013) *People and Performance*, Routledge, London

Kelly, B (2003) *Worth Repeating*, Kregel, Grand Rapids, MI

Ritson, M (2016) Maybe it's just me, but shouldn't an 'expert' in marketing be trained in marketing? *Marketing Week*, 12 July [Online] https://www.marketingweek.com/2016/07/12/mark-ritson-maybe-its-just-me-but-shouldnt-an-expert-in-marketing-be-trained-in-marketing/ [accessed 12 February 2017]

Chapter 9

Barta, T and Barwise, P (2017) *The 12 Powers of a Marketing Leader: How to succeed by building customer and company value*, McGraw-Hill, London

DaveStevensNow (2017) DaveStevensNow [blog] https://davestevensnow.com/ [accessed 22 March 2017]

Drucker, P F (1954) *The Practice of Management*, Harper, New York

Drucker, P F (1988; 2007) *The Essential Drucker: Selections from the management works of Peter F Drucker*, Elsevier, Oxford

English. Oxford Living Dictionaries (2017) [Online] https://en.oxforddictionaries.com/ [accessed 16 March 2017]

Goffee, R and Jones, G (2006) *Why Should Anyone Be Led by YOU? What it takes to be an authentic leader*, Harvard Business Review Press, Boston, MA
Grote, D (2017) 3 popular goal-setting techniques managers should avoid, *Harvard Business Review* [Online] https://hbr.org/2017/01/3-popular-goal-setting-techniques-managers-should-avoid [accessed 18 February 2017]
Marketing Charts (2016) CMOs say they want to spend their time on strategy [Online] http://www.marketingcharts.com/traditional/cmos-say-they-want-to-spend-their-time-on-strategy-72869 [accessed 12 December 2016]
Mindtools (2017) What is leadership? [blog] [Online] https://www.mindtools.com/pages/article/newLDR_41.htm [accessed 15 February 2017]
Stein IAS (2014) Great expectations: what today's CEOs expect from their marketers [Online] http://www.steinias.com/ceo [accessed 17 February 2017]
Udall, N (2014) *Riding the Creative Rollercoaster*, Kogan Page, London

Chapter 10

Allen, R (2016) What is programmatic marketing? Smart Insights, 3 February [Online] http://www.smartinsights.com/internet-advertising/internet-advertising-targeting/what-is-programmatic-marketing/ [accessed 19 February 2017]
English. Oxford Living Dictionaries (2017) [Online] https://en.oxforddictionaries.com/ [accessed 16 March 2017]
Young, J (1988) *Steve Jobs: The journey is the reward*, Scott Foresman, Glenview, IL

Chapter 11

Forsman & Bodenfors (2015) Grand prix for creative effectiveness [Online] http://www.fb.se/news/grand-prix-for-creative-effectiveness [accessed 9 February 2017]
Volvo (2012; 2015) Volvo Group Annual Report [Online] http://www.volvogroup.com/en-en/investors/reports-and-presentations/annual-reports.html [accessed 18 March 2017]
Volvo Trucks (2013) *The Epic Split* feat. Van Damme (Live Test) [video], YouTube [Online] http://www.youtube.com/watch?v=M7FIvfx5J10 [accessed 09 February 2017]
Volvo Trucks (2015) *Look Who's Driving* feat. 4-year-old Sophie (Live Test) [video], YouTube [Online] https://www.youtube.com/watch?v=7kx67NnuSd0 [accessed 9 February 2017]

Conclusion

Dead Poets Society (1989) Directed by Peter Weir, TouchStone Pictures
Young, J (1988) *Steve Jobs: The journey is the reward*, Scott Foresman, Glenview, IL

INDEX

Note: page numbers in italic indicate figures or tables.

3D marketing 73–90 *see also* 3D Marketing System for Strategy and Planning
- applied to business strategy 88–89
- as a business growth strategy 89–90 *see also* case studies

3D Marketing System for Strategy and Planning 73–88, 89, *74*
- differentiate, develop and deliver 74
- eight-step marketing planning framework 84–88, *84*
  - 1. purpose and objectives 84
  - 2. business and market context 85
  - 3. target audience(s) 85
  - 4. programme/campaign tactics and channels 85–86
  - 5. timeline 86
  - 6. resources 86–87
  - 7. measure and evaluate 87
  - 8. think different, do different 88
- the marketing plan and its go-to-market ecosystem 81–84, *83*
- strategy: four-step framework – goals, why, where and how 75–81, *75*
  - 1. articulating our goal 75–77
  - 2. articulating our why: three stonecutters story 77–78
  - 3. articulating our where 78
  - 4. articulating our how 78–80
  - put together – the strategic narrative 80–81, *80*, *81*

the 4Cs for customer perspective 107, *108*, 111–12, 115, 116–17

the 4Ps of the marketing mix (and) 106–07, *107*, 109, 112–15
- the 4Cs for customer perspective 107, *108 see also subject entry*
- the 7Ps of the services marketing mix 107, *108 see also subject entry*
- product, price, place and promotion 109
- reinterpreting for B2B marketing 112–14, *112*
  - 1. people instead of product or customers 112–13
  - 2. purpose instead of price or cost 113
  - 3. presence instead of place or convenience 114
  - 4. point of view/proposition instead of promotion or communication 114

The 7 Habits of Highly Effective People 125

the 7Ps of the services marketing mix 107, *108*, 110–11, 115

The 12 Powers of a Marketing Leader 149

Ali, M 44

all that glitters *see* tools, tactics and B2B marketing

Angelou, M 18

Apple 53
- and 'Think Different' campaign (1997) 9, 43–45 *see also* case studies

articles/papers (on)
- CEOs (*Forbes*, 2016) *see also* Pontefract, D 59
- 'The development of the science of marketing: an exploratory survey' (*Journal of Marketing*, 1945) 117
- 'Humans have shorter attention span than goldfish, thanks to smartphones' (*Telegraph*, 2015) 31
- leaders (Mindtools, 2017) 141
- McCarthy's 4Ps (*Advertising Age*, 1990) 111 *see also* Lauterborn, R F
- marketing (*Marketing Week*, 2016) 129 *see also* Ritson, M
- marketing myopia (*Harvard Business Review*, 1960) 24 *see also* Levitt, T
- 'The new marketing myopia' (*Journal of Public Policy & Marketing*) 25 *see also* Smith, C; Drumwright, M E *and* Gentile, M C
- purpose (*Forbes*, 2015) 59 *see also* Wartzman, R
- 'A refresher on marketing myopia' (*Harvard Business Review*, 2016) 24 *see also* Gallo, A
- Unilever's strategic principles (*Marketing Week*; LinkedIn) 92 *see also* Weed, K

Australia, content marketing in 35

B2B marketers, paradox for 29
B2B marketing: doing different (and) 91–98
see also case studies: Coca-Cola and Unilever
essential steps to *do different* 94–96
five habits to nurture 95
five questions and five actions 95, *96*
a return to marketing 93–94
B2B marketing, thinking differently about 43–48 *see also* case studies
essential steps to *think different* 47–48
five habits to nurture 47–48
five questions and five actions 48, *48*
B2B marketing basics 51–71
the brand conundrum in B2B (and) 53–59
brands with purpose – the Why matters 55–59, *57*
understanding purpose – Why? 53–55, *54*, *55*, *56*
customer engagement 65–68
and customer experience – the difference 66–68
the end of ROI as we know it? (and) 68–71
resetting the 'value' agenda 68–69
zero-based budgeting (ZBB) 70–71 *see also subject entry*
four fundamentals for success 51–52
the strategy imperative (and) 59–65
difference between strategy and plans 60–61
six questions separating strategy and plans 61–62
strategy as hard for B2B marketers – and obstacles 62–63
your marketing strategy and team meeting exercise 64–65
Barta, T (and) 149–50
the '12 Powers' 150
the Value Creation Zone (V-Zone) 150
Barwise, P (and) 149–50
the '12 Powers' 150
the Value Creation Zone (V-Zone) 150
Basic Marketing: A managerial approach 106–07
being better B2B marketers (and) 183–85
purpose-driven marketing 183–84
tactics and ideas for 184
thinking, being and doing different 184–85
being different in B2B marketing 175–81 *see also* case studies
being B2B marketers 177–78
essential steps to *be different* 179–71, *180–81*
Benioff, M (CEO, Salesforce.com) 56
Bitner, M J 110
BLP *see* case studies: purpose of marketing
Booms, B H 110
Borden, N 106, 107
Brenner, M 29
Business Marketing Club (BMC) 137
Bussell, D 115
and lesson for B2B marketers: learn the technique well 115

Canada Post 29 *see also* studies *and* TrueImpact
case studies (for/on)
B2B marketing: Unilever's four strategic principles 91–92
being different in B2B marketing: Volvo's Live Test series 175–77
and what B2B marketers can learn from Volvo 177
a business growth strategy 89–90
doing different: Coca-Cola Content 2020 initiative 96–98
and what B2B marketers can learn from Coca-Cola 98
purpose of marketing: not 'boring' B2B 118–21
Berwin Leighton Paisner (BLP) 120–21
IBM 119–20
Schneider Electric 118–19, 121
thinking differently about B2B marketing: Apple's 'Think Different' campaign 43–45
and what B2B marketers can learn on brand, strategy and customers 44–45
change (and) 9–22 *see also* definitions
client vs customer in B2B marketing 14–16
dealing with (who moved my cheese?) 20–21, *20*
emotions in B2B marketing 16–19, *18*, 32–33
the engagement continuum 12–14, *13*
how B2B marketers are responding to change 21–22
rise of social media 19–20
as seismic shift – in perspective 9–12
fundamental change in customer journey 10–11
beyond the sales funnel 11–12, *12*
Coca-Cola *see also* case studies: doing different
Content 2020 Initiative 35
Share a Coke campaign 39

Coleman-Smith, A (BLP, Marketing Director) 121
content marketing 34–36 *see also* Coca-Cola; definitions *and* reports
as failing and distracting marketers 35–36
Content Marketing Institute 35 *see also* reports
Converse, P D 117
Covey, S 125–27
Culliton, J 106
customer engagement *see also* customer engagement for the social era
and customer experience 66–68
lasting 5
customer engagement for the social era 157–73
five top tips for developing a big idea 167–73
1. make it human 167–68 *see also* National Health Service (NHS)
2. become social businesses 168–70
five top tips for 170–71
3. captivate the wider business upfront 171
4. take some risks 172
5. what comes next? 172–73
six rules for social engagement 158–65
1. start by listening 158–59
2. stop pushing 159–61
3. the 'so-what' factor 161–62
4. be responsive 162
5. do it and keep on doing it 163–64
6. quality not quantity 164–65
taking a big idea to market (by) 165–67
creating the big idea 165–67 *see also* National Health Service (NHS)
customer experience 66–68

Davies, A 2
definitions (of)
affinity 145
agility 145
authenticity (Hofmann, Y) 144
authenticity 144
client 15
content marketing (Content Marketing Institute) 35
customer 15
customer experience (*Harvard Business Review*) 40, 66
customer experience (Manning, H) 66
leaders (Mindtools) 141
personal 39
personas (Hubspot, 2016) 38
personalize 39
purpose 106
respond 162
responsive 162
social 159–60
Deighton, J 24–25
different: think, do and be different 3
'Digital is Dead' (Pritchard, M) 36
doing different *see* B2B marketing: doing different
Dowden, C 59
Drucker, P 129, 141, 154
and Management by Objectives (MBO) concept 154–55 *see also* SMART
Drumwright, M E 25

Einstein, A 44
e-mail 27, 29–30, 128
emotion *see also* Plutchik, R
colour wheel of 17, *18*
theory of 17

Facebook 19, 157, 163
face-to-face 27, 29, 137
Fahy, J 116
fallacies (for)
'be different' 99
'do different' 49
'think different' 7
figures
3D go-to-market ecosystem *83*
3D marketing planning framework *84*
3D marketing strategy *75*
3D Marketing System for B2B Strategy and Planning *74*
the 4Ps for B2B marketing *112*
the 4Ps of the marketing mix *107*
the 7Ps of the services marketing mix and the 4Cs of the customer-focused marketing mix *108*
the engagement continuum *13*
the Golden Circle *54*
the handwriting on the wall *20*
marketing process, inside-out *55*
marketing process, outside-in *56*
purpose, mission, vision and goal *57*
the sales funnel yesterday and today *12*
SMART objectives *155*
time management for B2B marketers *128*
wheel of emotion (Plutchik) *18*
Fonteyn, M 115
Foundations of Marketing 116

Gallo, A 24, 25
Gentile, M C 25
Goffee, R 142

Golden Circle of Why, How and What *54*, *54–55*, 93 *see also* Sinek, S
Goodall, J 44
Google 79, 116, 119, 141
Analytics 131
Graham, M 44
great B2B marketers (and) 123–40
career in marketing – advice (to my younger self) on 139–40
four essential qualities of 123–25
1. curiosity 123–24
2. thinking beyond marketing 124
3. willingness to challenge 124
4. customer perspective 124–25
debate on qualifications 129–38
attending conferences 135–37
five reasons for 136–37
networking 137–38
eight critical reasons for 138
qualified for B2B marketing? 130–32
reasons for marketers to have an MBA 132–34
seven behaviours of the most successful 125–29
1. have a strategy 125
2. take time to plan and execute brilliantly 125
3. start by listening 126
4. engage/synergize 126
5. take risks/be proactive 126
6. evaluate (think win-win) 126
7. be curious and learn from everyone 126–27
and use of time 127–29, *128*
Greenburg, P 66
Grote, D 155

Hofmann, Y 143–44

IBM 121
centennial film 166–67

Jobber, D 116
Jobs, S 43–44, 45, 164
Johnson, S 20
Jones, G 142
Just So Stories (Kipling) 61

Kanter, R M 113
Kennedy, J F 59
key takeaway for B2B marketers (leadership dilemma) 146
Kipling, R 61

Latham, G P 155
Lauterborn, R F 111–12, 116
leaders as time-rich 146
leadership dilemma in B2B marketing (on) 141–56
becoming B2B marketing leaders (and/by) 149–56, *155*
the '12 Powers' 150
leading and structuring our teams 150–53
objective-setting 154–56, *155* *see also* MBO *and* SMART
providing clarity 153–54
the Value Creation Zone (V-Zone) 150
CEOs: what they want from marketing 147–48 *see also* Stein, T
key takeaways for B2B marketers 146
marketing: should it have a seat on the board? 141–42
what makes a B2B marketing leader? 148–49
why should anyone be led by you? 142–47 *see also* marketing leadership
Levitt, T 24, 25
Lingqvist, O 13
LinkedIn 163
Marketing Solutions Technology business 103
Locke, E A 155
Lun Plotkin, C 13

MacDonald, J 3
McCarthy, E J 106
and 4Ps model 109, 110–15, *112*
McKinsey Quarterly (2015) 13–14
McKinsey recommendations and author's thoughts 13–14
Macreadie, B (Head of Brand and Campaign Marketing, BLP) 120–21
Management by Objectives (MBO) 154–55 *see also* Drucker, P *and* SMART
Manning, H 66 *see also* definitions
and 'How customers perceive their interactions with your company' 66
marketing at the core 2–3
marketing fundamentals 4–5
differentiate, develop, deliver for lasting customer engagement 5
strategy 4
and three fallacies of B2B marketing 4–5
marketing leadership 142–45
creation of 'next practice', not just 'best practice' 145
requirements for 143–44
capability development 144

performance management 144
stakeholder engagement 144
strategic direction 144
vision 143
three As for: authenticity, agility and affinity 144–45 *see also* definitions
marketing myopia 24–25, 46, *48*
Marketing Week 28
Master in Business Administration (MBA) 132–34, 140
Mathieu, M 91–92
Mildenhall, J (Coca-Cola) 97
model(s)
4Cs 111–12, 116
4Ps 109, 110–15, *112*
7Ps 110–11
eight-step planning 84, 85–88, *84*
marketing myopia 24–25, 46
sales funnel as 11–12, *12*
Morton, B 31

National Health Service (NHS)
campaign 166–68
foundation of 165–66

Plutchik, R (and) 17
theory of emotion 17
colour wheel of emotion 17, *18*
Polman, P (CEO, Unilever) 58
Pontefract, D 59
The Power of Words (video) 32–33
The Practice of Management 154
Pritchard, M (Proctor & Gamble): 'Digital is Dead' 36
the purpose of marketing (and) 101–22
dearth of creativity in B2B 117–18
and C for creativity 117–18
lead generation 102–03
the marketing mix revisited (and) 106–07, 109–17, *107*, *108*, *112*
4Cs for B2B marketing: clarity, credibility, consistency, competitiveness 116–17, 115
4Cs for customer perspective: customer, cost, convenience, communication 111–12, 114–15
7Ps of the services marketing mix 110–11, 115
marketing as a dance: ballerina's lesson for B2B marketers 114–16
reinterpreting the 4Ps for B2B marketing 112–14 *see also* the 4Ps
not 'boring' B2B 118–22 *see also* case studies
rediscovering our creativity – three lessons to learn 121–22
story of the three stonecutters revisited 103–04
threefold purpose 105–06
to build, maintain and protect the brand 105
customer engagement 105
to drive demand 106

reports (on)
B2B Content Marketing Benchmarking (Content Marketing Institute 2017) 35
'CXcellence: how to achieve CX success in B2B 2016–17' (B2B Marketing/ Circle Research) 40
'Great Expectations': understanding perspectives of B2B CEOs 147 *see also* Stein, T
'High Performance B2B Marketing' (2016) 51–52, 65
'How does digital affect Canadian attention spans?' (Microsoft, 2015) 30
marketing leaders (CMO Council and Deloitte) 147–48
'The path to 2020: marketers seize the customer experience' (Marketo, 2016) 40
television as dominant medium for marketing (Adobe Digital Index, 2016) 29
research (on)
B2B CEOs: 'Great Expectations' 147 *see also* Stein, T
customer satisfaction (Salesforce 2016 State of Marketing) 40
return on investment (ROI) 28, 29, 36, 52, 68–71, 87, 93, 103, 126
Riding the Creative Rollercoaster 145
Ritson, M 28, 37, 51, 85, 129–30, 131

Schneider Electric *see* case studies
Schulz, C M 158
and Peanuts 158
Schwabish, J 30
serendipity 160–61
Sinek, S 53–54, *54*, *55*, *56*, 93 *see also* Golden Circle
SMART – specific, measurable, achievable, realistic, timebound 155–56, *155*
Smith, C 25

social engagement *see* customer engagement for the social era
social media 163–64
  rise of 19–20
Sorrell, Sir M 29
Stanley, J 13
Start with Why: How great leaders inspire everyone to take action 53–54
Stein, T 147
  and Great Expectations: result of research into B2B CEOs 147
Stevens, D (CMO) 152
story of the three stonecutters 77–78, 103–04
study of the brain's response to different marketing tactics/channels (TrueImpact) 29–30
surveys (on)
  CEOs globally (PwC, 2016) 57–58
  lead generation as primary goal for B2B marketers (Content Marketing Institute (2017) 103
Szent-Györgyi, A 140

tables
  be different Q&A *180–81*
  do different Q&A *96*
  the strategic narrative *80*
  the strategic narrative: example *81*
  think different Q&A 48
Terling, L (Volvo Trucks, VP of Marketing and Communication) 177
Thought Expansion Network 3
time management 127–29 *see also* Covey, S
tools, tactics and B2B marketing (and) 23–41
  magpie mania: focusing our marketing (and/through) 33–41 *see also* definitions
    from Big Data to analytics 37–38
    'buyer personas' 38–39
    content marketing 34–36 *see also subject entry*
    customer experience (CX) as new customer centricity 39–41 *see also* reports
    digital and social media marketing 36–37
    personalization or personal – a difference? 39
    storytelling 34
  'marketing myopia' 24–27 *see also* articles/papers; Deighton, J *and* Gallo, A
    B2B 25–27
    'new' 25
  traditional vs new (digital) marketing *see subject entry*; case studies *and* TrueImpact
traditional vs new (digital) marketing (and) 27–33
  attention span, fall in 30–32
    goldfish statistic 30–31 *see also* articles *and* reports
    myth of 31–32
    the power of words 32–33
  research statistics for 29
TrueImpact
  study of the brain's response to different marketing tactics/channels 29–30
  white paper: *A Bias for Action*: four key findings 29–30
Twitter 19, 129, 158–59, 160, 162, 163, 170

Udall, N (CEO, 'nowhere') (and) 145–46
  description of *Innovation* 146
  'Leaders are time-rich' 146
  Riding the Creative Rollercoaster 145
Unilever 58–59 *see also* case studies: B2B marketing
  and zero-based budgeting (ZBB) approach 70
United Kingdom (UK)
  conferences in 135
  content marketing in 35
  legislation: Health and Social Care Act 166
United States (US)
  CEOs in 57–58 *see also* surveys
  content marketing in 35

Vizard, S 2016 29
Volvo *see* case studies: being different in B2B marketing

Wartzman, R 59
Weed, K 92
Weir, M 103
what makes a great B2B marketer? *see* great B2B marketers
Who Moved My Cheese? 20
Why Should Anyone Be Led by You? 142
words, the power of 32–33
Wright, F L 44

zero-based budgeting (ZBB) (and) 70–71
  accountability 71
  changing perceptions 70–71
  focus 71
  new ways of thinking 71